Camaro

Camaro

JAMES A. DIETZLER

MetroBooks

MetroBooks

An Imprint of Friedman/Fairfax Publishers

Library of Congress Cataloging-in-Publication Data.

Dietzler, Jim.
    Camaro / Jim Dietzler.
        p.   cm.
    Includes bibliographical references and index.
    ISBN 1-56799-816-X
    1. Camaro automobile—History.   I. Title.
TL215.C33D54   1999
629.222'2—dc21   99-35325
                                                                        CIP

Editor: Ann Kirby
Art Director: Kevin Ullrich
Design: Robert Beards Design, Inc.
Photography Editor: Valerie E. Kennedy
Production Manager: Richela Fabian

Color separations by Spectrum Pte Ltd.
Printed in Hong Kong by Sing Cheong Printing Company Ltd.

10 9 8 7 6 5 4 3 2

For bulk purchases and special sales, please contact:
Friedman/Fairfax Publishers
Attention: Sales Department
15 West 26th Street
New York, NY 10010
212/685-6610 FAX 212/685-1307

Visit our website:
www.metrobooks.com

Dedication:

To My Parents.
For all of their support and faith over the years.

Acknowledgments:

Putting together a historical account of a single automobile such as this entailed the dedicated hard work and efforts of many individuals who work in a multitude of fields directly and indirectly related to the automotive arena. Though I can't thank them enough for their help, I'd like to express my appreciation for their contributions; if anyone is omitted, my apologies.

First off, I'd like to thank my former colleague Richard Lentinello for tossing my name into the ring when an author was being sought, and for having the confidence in my abilities to do so.

The following former and present GM employees made themselves available (sometimes unknowingly and without prior introduction) to me, and provided data, contacts, and interviews: Tom Hoxie, Ralph Kramer, Mark Leddy, Julie Pevos, Joel M. Scheuher, Erica Strackbein, and Carol Waldowski.

Peter Hylton, the SCCA's historial archivist, is a gentleman who handles a vast treasure trove of American road-racing information. A big thank-you for responding to my inquiries in a prompt and professional manner, and for tolerating those odd-hour phone calls to provide the answer to that one question I didn't come up with the first time around.

At Michael Friedman Publishing reside an immensely talented pool of individuals who took the rough edges off and polished the package I gave them into the fine book you have in front of you. My hat's off to copyeditor Diane Boccadoro, photo editor Valerie Kennedy, and editor Ann Kirby.

On a final note, this project likely would have ground to a standstill if it wasn't for the sometimes gentle proddings from my fiancée, Kristie. Tolerating stacks of mildewed magazines from my collection, late nights in front of the computer, the entire takeover with research materials of our shared home office, and the incessant ringing of the phone at all hours—she put up with everything, and for that gets my sincere apologies and gratitude.

Contents

Introduction

Little did I know at the time just how intricately my later life would become so entwined with the car that I did more than admire—for which I lusted, I craved, and I dreamed. At the time, though, and still, fourteen-year-olds weren't allowed to drive (unless they lived on a farm). No, all I could do during my early high school years was go along for the ride as my buds and I crammed into the back of an older friend's '69 RS/SS convertible. That bad beauty was Glacier Blue, sported a white interior and top, and 396 cubes under the hood. Of course, it wasn't a dead stocker either; in those days, the opinion was that if it didn't have a hot lopey cam, Hooker headers, cherry bombs or glass packs, and a set of Cragar SSes or Torque Thrusts Ds, it wasn't even worth a second look.

Even before that time, I can recall the days in the mid- to late '70s when my older brother and I used to prowl the streets of our grandmother's Pennsylvania coal-region town, on the lookout for hot Camaros. He'd invariably ask me which ones I thought had the performance, and at my young age, I'd always look at stripes and spoilers and pick the wrong ones (as if there can be a wrong Camaro). He at least knew how to recognize performance based on the engine emblems on the fenders.

In the mid- to late '80s, the family driveway was home to my brother's first-generation F-body—which he seemed to hate, or at least that's the way he drove it. Not a month went by that I wasn't helping him bolt in yet another junkyard engine, trans, or rear end. Of course, before I ever got behind the wheel, he'd blow it to pieces and we'd start over again. When he got involved in the collision repair business, there were plenty of wrecked third-generation Camaros to rebuild and sell, and it seemed there was always a Camaro in the driveway.

Today, my experience with the latest Camaros comes from my ties to the automotive world as an automotive journalist. Though many things in the industry have changed, one has remained true—the love of enthusiasts for the Camaro. It isn't hard to spot either. Just head out to a local cruise-in spot or hit a local car show. The early F-cars that inspired several generations are still with us, in many cases in better condition how than when they came from the factory, the mag wheels gone, replaced with the correct stock rims, as are the rest of the aftermarket parts that were bolted on early in their lives. Out at the dragstrips, Camaros of all four generations are chosen by racers who know a good thing when they see it and alone are worth the price of admission to watch.

As far as collectibility is concerned, the Camaro enjoys favored status among the many ponycars and musclecars produced during the '60s and '70s. This is due in part to the huge aftermarket offering of parts. Everything from engines to sheetmetal to upholstery can be had for a vintage Camaro, allowing restorers to bring many a rusted-out shell back to life. Across the country Chevrolet car shows draw perhaps the largest crowds, in numbers of both participants and spectators. Out of all the models, you'll find that Camaros usually present the strongest showing, and for good reason.

When the offer to author this history of the Camaro came my way, it was a no-brainer to accept. Unfortunately, many of those involved with the early Camaros are no longer with us, including first-generation designer Henry "Hank" Haga, Vince Piggins, whose efforts brought us the legendary 302-Z28 package, and William Mitchell, then GM's vice president, whose attitude toward performance led to some of the hottest cars ever to roll out of Detroit.

This isn't a numbers-crunching book for those looking to verify originality, nor is it an all-out listing of every possible option and combination thereof. Rather, it's the story of America's favorite ponycar, written for those who know everything about the Camaro as well as those who know next to nothing about it. Enjoy it for what it is, the tale of a wonderful creation that has meant so much to so many.

PAGE 6: Dog-dish hubcaps, no stripes, no engine-related badging—the ultimate sleeper. The only giveaway that this particular 1969 Camaro had the potential to blow your doors off is the cowl-induction ZL-2 hood, beneath which lies hidden the most desirable engine to come off of GM's production lines, the all-aluminum 427-cubic-inch ZL-1. OPPOSITE: With its NACA ducted hood and stylish striping, the 1979 Z28 continued to hold the line on visual impact. The return to performance, however, was still a good ways down the road.

Rising to the Challenge

GM's First Ponycar Battles Its Big Three Rivals

The decade was the 1960s; the scene was Main Street, Anytown, U.S.A.; and the targets were performance-minded automotive enthusiasts, preferably young, employed gearheads who could afford new cars. Some had parents with similar inclinations, who had lifted themselves out of the anxieties of World War II by cobbling together whatever old body shells and engines could be culled from the junkyards scattered across the land, creating cheap, sometimes dangerous hot rods that satiated their need for speed. But America's latest speed-inclined teenagers were coming of age in a new automotive marketplace. What did the trick in the '50s and early '60s—bucket Ts, deuce coupes, and the like—belonged to another generation, an older generation that *this* generation was intent on distancing itself from. Rock 'n roll with a psychedelic edge was displacing the doo-wop sounds, and on the streets Detroit's machines were beginning to roll off the dealership floors primed and ready with high-performance engines, smooth aerodynamic styling, and bright colors aimed at what was to become known in the industry as the "youth market."

In the decade that saw the first of the musclecars—basically preexisting business coupes packaged with potent engines—corporate rivalries soon filtered down to the streets. Pontiac fired the first shot with its 389-equipped Tempest, the GTO. Other manufacturers soon followed: Ford with the Fairlane 500, Chrysler with its 1966 Dodge Charger and later the Plymouth Belvedere-based Road Runners, and Chevy with the Chevelle SSes. The first of what would become known affectionately as the ponycar came from GM's rivals, Ford and Chrysler. A ponycar took the musclecar tradition and infused it with a better sense of styling, adding smooth flowing looks to power. Ponycars were more sporty grand touring cars than true sports cars. Though they are often used interchangeably, there's a distinct difference between the terms *ponycar* and *musclecar*, one of looks and target audience. The ponycar carried the European tradition of the sports car a step further than the tiny two-seat affairs that had come from across the water in the 1950s. The musclecar didn't need the styling cues, just the raw power.

For its version of the ponycar, Ford took its intermediate-sized Falcon and gave it a major sheetmetal massage and introduced the 1964 $^1/_2$ Mustang in April of that year amid some major promotional hoopla. The Mustang's standard V6 powerplant delivered less than adequate power for those concerned with straightline speed, but an optional 289-cubic-inch V8 engine could be had and was selected by a large majority of the more than 250,000 Mustang buyers that year. In May 1964, Chrysler's Plymouth automotive branch, in a somewhat more quiet manner, introduced to the motoring public its small 2+2-styled performance car, the Barracuda, a two-door coupe with a fastback greenhouse and 235-hp four-barrel carbureted 273-cubic-inch V8.

OPPOSITE: A 1968 SS Camaro gleams in Matador Red. This raging bull is otherwise interpreted as Street Screamer. In addition to the distinctive pinstriping, the SS package offered a wide range of high-power engines to chose from.

Though not known for nimble cornering when optioned with the heavy V8 engines, these cars could get from point A to point B, in most cases from stoplight to stoplight, as fast as or faster than many homebuilt hot rods. This of course left the homebuilt hot rodders shaking their heads with a touch of frustration: they had built an entirely new segment of the automotive market with their own sweat, skinned knuckles, and ingenuity, and in a short time the kids could just drop their dimes and drive off with hi-po machines! Of course, not too long after these street-scorching contraptions began to appear, the speed shops and aftermarket parts manufacturers began to tap into this new market. Those lacking the cash for high-power options did like their hot rodding forebears: they built the power they couldn't buy.

Above: A 1967 Camaro, optioned with the legendary RPOZ28 302-cubic-inch small-block derived from the Trans-Am race effort, was another wolf in sheep's clothing, albeit in tuxedo-black sheep's skin! Right: The interior of this 1968 SS 396 carries the "jet age" look that was *en vogue* at the time, with its "stirrup" shifter, sawtooth auxil-

Where was GM while its competitors were reaping the benefits of an altogether untapped market? It was banking on two cars in its product line, neither of which stood a fair chance compared to the newly styled machines the competition was then offering. Chevrolet's 1964 Malibu and Impala SS, though similar to Ford's and Chrysler's latest machines in that they were two-door hardtop sports coupes, lacked the fastback design and eye-catching appeal of the Barracuda and Mustang. In the eyes of the teens on the street, they were Mom's and Dad's hot rods. They were, in a word, square!

Of course, Chevy did have the Corvette, a two-place sports car available in both coupe and convertible forms, but this was a car for the upper crust, and its rival was Ford's "personal" car, the Thunderbird. Chevrolet also had its Corvair, the rear-engined six-cylinder model that had been around since 1959. Its rivals were the Ford Falcon, from which the Mustang evolved, and the Plymouth Valiant, the design from which the Barracuda was derived. By 1964, the Corvair had already been named Car of the Year at least once by the automotive press, and it offered excellent handling for its day. But because of its unconventional design and drivetrain layout, it didn't do as well as its rivals in sales and was later found to be more expensive to produce than the F-car-based Camaro. It was also the car that fueled government scrutiny of the automotive industry after Ralph Nader lambasted its handling characteristics in his 1966 book, *Unsafe at Any Speed*.

Realizing the need to play catch-up with Ford, Chevrolet's design and engineering teams began work in late 1964 on what would become the F-car platform. Former GM public relations director Ralph Kramer (1986–93) explained the car's birth as "a knee-jerk reaction to the Mustang. A bunch of people got together as a committee, and through their talents, created the Camaro. There wasn't any real market research. Bill Mitchell [then GM's vice president of design] would just take off and visit spots where car guys got together with their hot rods. From a standpoint of taking a methodical approach to studying the market, like what was done with the later versions, that didn't happen."

At one point, the project looked as if it would hit the dealers' showroom floors bearing the name Panther. One likely reason for the name change to Camaro — aside from Chevrolet's penchant for using words starting with the letter *C* — was the fact that Mercury was set to unveil a new car for 1967, the Cougar. Panther and Cougar were just a little too close in image for comfort.

In the two very short years that it took to bring the Camaro to market, GM and Chevrolet did their homework and did it well. And by the time the car was introduced, there were more than just two rivals to deal with. The Camaro would need to be able to stand its ground, which is no small task for a new model. By 1967, Chrysler's famous (or infamous, depending upon whose opinion you're soliciting) Street Hemi was already several years into the game, delivering NASCAR and Super Stock drag racing performance to those who could afford the extra cash for the optional 450-hp engine. Likewise, Ford was into the big-cubic-inch scene, offering its buyers a 428-cubic-inch big-block to stuff under the hood of the Mustang.

Unlike Chrysler's and Ford's offerings, though, Chevrolet's Camaro was an all-new design from the ground up, based on an undercarriage that had no rival. The Mustang had debuted with a fully unitized body shell, in that stamped steel panels were joined together without a perimeter or ladder-style frame, and the suspension components were hung off reinforced sections of the unibody, as that style chassis came to be known. The drawbacks to the unibody design stemmed directly from the stamped steel sheetmetal's lack of lasting structural integrity. Hard cornering under power translated into shock tower flex. Major stresses transmitted directly to the body shell and into the thin sheetmetal, ensuring that, over time, fractures would begin to appear through the paintwork in highly stressed areas. Often, critical components such as shock and spring mounts would wear at the metal, allowing component movement, which directly affected a car's handling performance. To alleviate this design flaw, the hi-po 289 Mustangs would all come with shock tower struts, reinforcing bars that eliminated much of the flex. In convertible ver-

The buyer of this 1967 RS/SS 396 convertible got the best of three worlds: luxurious styling, a unique look via the RS option, and the brute big-block power of the SS 396.

sions, the chassis warranted even further support, with a large plate affixed below the transmission for added strength.

Not so for the Camaro. From the first day of its phenomenal life, the Camaro used a front subframe to which its front suspension components and engine were mounted. The subframe was produced using thick-gauge steel and was closed or boxed in on all four sides. A metal-sandwiched rubber "biscuit" between the subframe and the underside of the Camaro's body isolated the vibrations that transmitted through the subframe from both the road and drivetrain components.

In essence, the rear shell of the car, built by the Fisher Body Division (hence the familiar Body By Fisher sill plates in GM products), was constructed in a unibody manner with stamped steel sections welded together. Although in concept this was the same body shell process applied to the Mustang, Fisher's engineering staff saw to it that the Camaro's body was rigidly reinforced at all critical areas where the rear suspension mounted. This isolated road and drivetrain noise more effectively and better utilized available space.

It also was designed to include a revolutionary anticorrosion system known as the wash-and-dry rocker. Realizing that the rear of the hood and the base of the windshield were high-pressure air zones, the engineers took advantage of the incoming air by routing it through openings in the top of the cowl. From there, the air and any rainwater would be forced down through the sides of the cowl to its base, which opened directly into the rocker panels. The rockers had bottom vents in front of the rear quarter panels, where the incoming air would eventually force the water out. Though a sound engineering principle, the system's one disadvantage was that if one had to park an F-body car facing even slightly downhill, any water that gathered in the car while it was parked would sit at the base of the cowl. This made for many a rotted-out Camaro.

Despite that one drawback, the resulting body, which was intentionally designed to be slightly larger than the Mustang in nearly all dimensions, was a major success given the short period of development time with which the engineers and designers had to work. Combined with the front subframe system, the Camaro was immune from the forces that tore apart other fully unitized cars over time. Late in the platform's development, GM offered its Pontiac division the chance to develop its own version of the F-car, which became the Firebird. Though the first-generation designs of the two ponycars shared the same sheetmetal, that would be the only time, and later versions wouldn't offer the interchangeability that the first generation did.

GM's Pony Enters the Corral

After two years of hectic design work and performance analysis, Chevrolet's engineers and stylists saw their dreams fulfilled in September 1966. The first Camaros rolled off the assembly lines at Norwood, Ohio, and Van Nuys, California, and into the lives of the public amid excellent reviews from automotive journalists of the day. Its sleek, svelte styling carried enough of a European heritage to be recognizable, yet it was a wholly new car, matched by nothing else Detroit then had to offer. Its slightly curved roofline swept down at the rear, flowing seamlessly into the rear quarter panels directly above the rear wheels. A short decklid and long nose added further to the look inherited somewhat from the likes of Jaguar's E-type and other sports cars whose lineages came from other shores.

The angled belt line protruded from its flanks just on the centerline of the body, adding a muscular tone without bulging out in an unsightly fashion. A smaller flank line just above the rocker panels completed the look of what has been termed Coke-bottle styling. Constant-radius wheelwells continued the flowing, rounded look. Up front the grille carried a pair of headlamps that sat flush with the leading edges of the fenders, with parking lamps located in the grille inboard of the headlamps. The nose peaked at the center of the hood, and both the grille and the front chrome bumper followed the hood's line. There wasn't a secondary

OPPOSITE: This pair of 1967s show off the clean "Coke bottle" styling that made the Camaro an overnight success. Both wear the Bumblebee nose stripe. The convertible, an RS/SS, sports a 350-cubic-inch small-block under the hood while the coupe is another of the 396 big-blocks.

This 1967 Z28-optioned hardtop is one of 602 built that year. Note the simple headlight and grille design indicative of the inaugural year Camaros.

pillar to clutter the view of the side. Instead, the rear three-quarter window rose up and forward to set flush with the driver's and passenger's windows. At the rear, rectangular taillights sat above the slim chrome bumper, the reverse lights were centered under the taillights below the bumper, and the tail was balanced with a centrally located fuel filler cap. In the eyes of the enthusiasts, the Camaro proudly displayed a look that was "just plain fast sitting still!"

The Camaro wasn't just an affordable street machine for motorheads, however. By offering buyers a wide variety of options with which to style their cars, even the first models could be ordered in such a way that, side by side, two differently optioned Camaros would have very distinct appearances. The first-generation Camaro also had a tough market to step into in terms of powertrain options, and GM knew it. Looking fast sitting still was one thing; getting up to speed quickly and maintaining the upper hand on the streets of America was another. Unlike the Mustang, which debuted with one base engine and one optional engine, the Camaro could be had with a variety of powerplants, enough to satisfy everyone, from those with a soft touch seeking a timid, street-mannered powerplant to those who wanted a steel chariot that would scorch the streets and strips, leaving anyone who dared rise to the challenge muttering under his breath about store-bought speed.

Right off the bat, Chevrolet knew that the Camaro had to appeal to a wide segment of the buying public. The long list of items on its Camaro Convenience Options gave owners the ability to personalize the looks of their new rides, both inside and out.

More significantly, there were three performance package options that led to the creation of some of the most legendary and collectible musclecars of the era. When one ordered a Camaro (coupe only) with option code Z28 (which 602 people did in 1967), the result was a Camaro coupe fitted with a 302-cubic-inch V8, dual exhaust, heavy-duty suspension, heavy-duty radiator with a temperature-controlled cooling fan, quick-ratio steering, 3.73:1 rear gearing, 15x6-inch (38x15cm) rims and 7.35x15-inch (19x38cm) red-stripe tires, and, for cosmetic identification, a pair of fat racing stripes running lengthwise over the hood and trunk. For the first two years of production, the Z28-optioned Camaro had no external callouts to note its special attributes other than the racing stripes. This would change in 1969, when Z28 badging was added to the option package.

However, you couldn't order option Z28 alone. The Muncie close-ratio four-speed transmission (option M21) and power brakes with front disc brakes had to be purchased as well. For those who absolutely wanted the baddest Z28-optioned Camaro in the land, Chevrolet was willing to throw in a few extra items, but you had to pay. Those items were a cross-ram intake manifold atop which two four-barrel carburetors were mounted, a specific ducting and air filter system to feed the air to the dual four-barrels, and a set of tubular exhaust headers. The interesting part was that upon delivery, if you looked under the hood of a Camaro optioned as such, you wouldn't see these items. They were shipped inside the trunk for the customer to install! Performance-wise, the cross-ram intake setup surprisingly wasn't the hottest ticket for bottom-end torque. Rather, it was designed to offer brute power at the mid- to upper levels of the powerband, something more suited for

road racing. It is likely that many buyers were shocked when they found themselves getting smoked off the line by a regular Z28-optioned Camaro with only a single four-barrel carburetor up top.

For those who wanted a racy look but not quite the neck-snapping acceleration of the Z28, there was the Rally Sport package (RS). With this option, the Camaro's nose was treated to a set of electrically activated pop-up "hideaway" headlights and a restyled grille, which required that the parking lights be moved to the metal valence panel below the front bumper. In addition, the RS included moldings on the lower body, blacked-out bezels around the taillights, chrome moldings around the wheelwells and roof drip rail, and RS badging in the grille and on the gas cap and fenders. Of course, what would a cosmetic option be without a set of stripes? For the RS, these were slim body-side pinstripes that ran from nose to tail.

Then there was the SS, sort of a combination appearance and power package that could be combined with the RS package, but not with option Z28. The SS option was little more than the buyer's choice of three high-performance V8s: the 350-cubic-inch V8 rated at 295 horsepower, a 396-cubic-inch 325-hp engine, or the top-rated big-block, a version of the 396 that provided 375 ponies for you to summon with a simple stab of your right foot. You just had to remember to tell the person riding shotgun to hang on, or it was a quick trip into the backseat! And to let everyone know just what was going on, SS badges were placed on the fenders, grille, and filler cap; there was also a special insulated hood with nonfunctional scoops, additional brightwork, and

Early Camaro emblems were innocuously styled, but the badging below the name, similiar to that of the Corvettes, spoke volumes about the car's potential.

Though this convertible sports '69 Z/28 badging on the fenders, the fully rounded wheel openings and sharply peaked grille are dead giveaways to its '68 vintage. BOTTOM: This 1967 RS sports the RPO Z22's trademark hideaway headlights and is an actual Z28-optioned production model. The side vent quarter windows were a one-year-only item.

shorter 14x6-inch (35.5x15cm) rims with red-stripe tires. Early production '67 SS models also received the Bumblebee stripe around the nose of the car, but later this was available as a separate option and didn't necessarily proclaim that one was packing a heavy hitter under the hood.

All told, there were seven different-displacement V6 and V8 engines planned for the Camaro, but not all of those made it into production. One that fell by the wayside was the 283-cubic-inch V8, which was used in a variety of cars in the Chevrolet product line from the Chevelle to the Corvette. Two V6 engines displacing 230 and 250 cubic inches offered up 140 and 155 horsepower, respectively. Then there were the V8s, four different displacements (302, 327, 350, and 396) that accounted for a total of six different performance levels. The base six-cylinder engine was the 230-cubic-incher, and the 155-hp Turbo Thrift Six was an option that added less than thirty dollars to the sticker. The base V8 was the 327-cubic-inch powerplant.

By taking the base 327 block and adding the crankshaft from the 283 engine, Chevrolet Engineering came up with a bore/stroke combination that displaced 302 cubic inches. This particular engine, which formed the basis of the previously mentioned Z28 option package, was a necessity borne out of the Sports Car Club of America's (SCCA) regulation that required the engines in production-based cars racing in its recently introduced Trans-Am class be limited to five liters (305 cubic inches). In order to participate in Trans-Am, it was mandated that both a car and engine be available as a regular offering from the automotive manufacturer or as an optional (a process known as homologation). By allowing the public to buy the Z28 package, Chevrolet was guaranteed victories, even if it was not openly supporting those racing the Z28 Camaros. Simply put: purpose-built racer for sale—see your local Chevrolet dealer! My, how times change.

The fact that the factory wasn't openly involved stemmed from a 1957 industry-wide AMA ban on racing participation, one that GM finally backed in 1963. "Win on Sunday, Sell on Monday" had become a marketing concept of the past. In truth, Chevrolet developed this engine with

the sole purpose of dislodging the Mustang from its reign as Trans-Am's king of the hill. And though the cars may not have been "factory-backed," clandestine factory support did make it to those racing Chevrolets, specifically Camaros in the Trans-Am series. In 1968 the Camaro would emerge the victor, thanks in no small part to the Z28 302 engine and the factory-engineered cross-ram induction system.

The 327 small-block was another tried-and-true Chevrolet small-block that was available with two different compression and induction/carburetion packages, producing 210 and 275 horsepower. Perhaps the longest-lived powerplant, if not in the industry then at General Motors, was the 350. In the 1967 Camaro, it was capable of producing 295 horsepower, and it lives on today in the latest versions of the car. Last, but certainly not least, was the only big-block ever shipped in a Camaro to the customer through normal channels: the 396-cubic-inch mill that initially, like the Z28 option package, was not available to the public when it was first unveiled. Though it had been around since 1965 in the Chevelle SS, its power level had dropped from a high of 375 horsepower to a 350-hp version in '67. When it came to the Camaro, though, three versions of the 396 could be had (325, 350, and 375 hp), all with a 10.25:1 compression ratio and four-barrel carburetion.

When it came to rear end gear ratios, Chevrolet liked to offer buyers a wide variety, just as it did with the engines. For those buying a Camaro with option Z28, the 3.73:1 ring-and-pinion set was a must. This was the highest ratio available and offered a good rate of acceleration for the stoplight warriors. Also available as regular options were 3.55:1, 3.31:1, 3.07:1, and 2.73:1 gearsets. For the economy-minded, the 2.73s were the way to go, of course. What made good sense for sustained highway speeds didn't exactly plant one back in the seat too well. Along with gear ratio choices, the optional Positraction rear differential ensured that the Camaro's power would be put down evenly on the asphalt. Surprisingly, nearly half of the Camaros sold with 275-plus-hp V8s came with non-Positraction "open" rear ends, meaning that one tire inevitably went up in a haze of smoke while the other sat basically motionless until traction

overcame the engine's acceleration and the car actually started moving forward.

Inside the Camaro, thirty individual options were available to allow the buyer to personalize his new sporty car. Of course, some options were mutually exclusive, like the Strato-Back bench seat and the floor-mounted console/shifter. Some were simply different versions of the same items, like radios. In addition to the individual options, either a special interior (Z23) or a custom interior (Z87) was offered. The special interior group came with chrome-trimmed brake, accelerator, and clutch pedals, as well as chrome-trimmed windshield pillars and roofrail moldings. These latter two moldings basically outlined the upper front two-thirds of the interior edge, where the door closed, with chrome.

The custom interior package went a little bit further, offering custom door panels with molded armrests and sunken door handles, lighting in the glove compartment and in the rear of the car on the sail panel behind the doors,

a Deluxe steering wheel, an ashtray and armrests for backseat passengers, and tasteful color-keyed accent stripes in the vinyl upholstery. Ten different colors allowed for some strange interior/exterior color combinations, and custom and standard seating qualities were offered for both bench and bucket seating arrangements, with specific colors reserved for each level. The only exception to the seat offerings, like several of the options, was that in convertibles the buyer could get only bucket seats.

To fire up this machine, one twisted an ignition key set to the right of the steering wheel in the dashboard, a feature that would last for just one more year. The speedometer and ancillary gauges were mounted dead inline with the driver's eyes in two separate round openings. Heater/AC and radio controls were centrally located, with an ashtray below, and the optional secondary gauge cluster mounted below the ashtray, making a continuous dash panel to the center console, if ordered as such. With this gauge option, the right-

Again we see a '68 Z28-optioned RS with '69 badging. This one also wears the stylish RPO D80 front chin and rear spoilers. Extensive brightwork was also part of RS option package.

hand combined gauge was replaced with a 7,000-rpm speedometer. If an 8-track tape player was ordered along with that secondary gauge cluster and center console, it went into an unlikely position on the rear of the console, where it could serve as a center armrest, albeit a hot one!

Outside, in addition to the previously mentioned performance and appearance packages, Chevrolet's paint department offered fifteen different colors to choose from. Several trim and stripe packages allowed buyers to create everything from a sparkling example of a stylist's exercise replete with contrasting stripes and interior to a bare-bones blacked-out stripper. Chevrolet, like most other automakers at the time, also offered vinyl roof coverings. However appealing to the eye, the tendency for moisture to "wick" under the vinyl coverings was the bane of many a Camaro, because it encouraged rust. Said vinyl roofs were either black or beige.

Perhaps the only negative trait of the '67s was the rear suspension arrangement, which was a carryover from previously existing Chevrolet models. A pair of single monoleaf springs at the rear supported the axle and rear end housing. Damping was provided by two shocks mounted behind the housing. The downfall of this system, particularly with the more powerful engines, was that when one stood on the gas hard from a dead stop, the resulting launch was quite unpleasant. When the tires stopped spinning enough to actually grab the pavement, they caused the rear end housing to rotate forward, inducing a windup of the leaf springs. This windup would then overpower the traction of the tires, resulting in a jarring shudder as the tires broke contact with the ground, the springs rebounded, and the process started again until one had gained enough momentum to actually begin rolling forward smoothly. The engineers attempted to correct this mechanical phenomenon, dubbed rear wheel hop, in the high-performance models and Z28-optioned cars with a traction bar mounted from underneath the axle tube to the underside of the chassis. This Band-Aid-type fix didn't really correct the problem.

For the following model year, the rear shocks were staggered, with the driver's-side shock mounted ahead of the axle tube. This provided a better solution, as the damping action of the shock slowed the rate of spring windup and rebound, allowing the tires to maintain traction in an alternate manner without making the rear end of the car feel as if it had just slammed over railroad tracks.

Looking back over the years, it's easy to see that Chevrolet knew it could sell the Camaro not only to its initial youth market target audience but also to others who wanted a sporty car for the weekends alongside the family wagon or sedan. One period Chevrolet advertisement for the 1967 Camaro displayed three very differently optioned versions of the car. First was the "Camaro about town," a coupe with bucket seats and a synchronized three-speed manual billed as "Especially nice for wife-types." Below it on the full-page spread was the "country club Camaro," a Rally Sport–optioned coupe with its trademark RS hideaway headlights and the standard V8, rated at 210 hp. For that version, the Chevy ad men told the buyer to "Decorate the right front seat suitably." And on the bottom of this none-too-subtle, across-the-boards marketing pitch was an SS convertible hailed as "Camaro the Magnificent." It packed a 396 big-block under the hood, a four-speed manual to transfer the power, and the rest of the SS decor package. The ad men didn't have to tell their audience who this ride was intended for; the ad just closed with "At your Chevrolet Dealer."

By the time the first model year run was finished, there was no doubt as to the success of the Camaro. More than 220,000, including just a tad over 25,000 convertibles, had sold, ranging from base six-cylinder coupes with a sticker just under $2,500 to optioned-out street killers that were nearly double that price.

Improving the Breed

For the 1968 models, Chevrolet stuck with its game plan, which had proven effective in the Camaro's introductory year. The exterior styling was a hit, and there were no serious changes in the bodylines. The vent windows in

The baddest of the bad! Painted in Cortez Silver, this '69 RS packs the legendary ZL-1 427-cubic-inch aluminum big-block. It's generally accepted that most of the 69 ZL-1 Camaros that made it into the hands of the public were special-ordered with one use in mind— drag strip domination.

the doors disappeared, and minor changes were made at the nose and tail. These two areas showed the most obvious changes, with the taillights divided into two sections via the external bezels. Though not as distinctive as the split grille made famous by Pontiac in the late '50s, the Camaro's nose took on a more defined look, with a grille that highlighted the angular peak at its center. The Rally Sport's electrically operated headlight doors were replaced with a more reliable vacuum system.

Most of the changes made to the 1968 model were mechanical in nature and, as with the early years of most recently introduced models, were done for the sake of improving the breed. As mentioned earlier, the traction bar solution for the rear wheel hop problem was a quick fix: the shock locations were staggered fore and aft of the rear axle. For the high-power V8s, with the exception of two versions of the 327, a multileaf rear spring pack replaced the single monoleaf spring. Also, for those with all-out performance in mind, four-wheel disc brakes could be ordered, but only through the dealer, and only as a dealer- or customer-installed option.

Perhaps one of the most desirable options available, aside from the top-performance V8, was the famed Muncie heavy-duty close-ratio four-speed gearbox (option code M22), otherwise known as the Rock Crusher. A beefed-up version of the close-ratio M21 four-speed, this gearbox could take the abuse of powershifting street and strip racers. One can usually tell when one is riding in an M21 or M22 four-speed-equipped ponycar by the higher-than-normal gear whine coming up through the transmission tunnel, and, in skilled hands, by the way the engine revs don't fall off in rpm between shifts. In clumsy hands, the gearbox lived up to its name by the clashing of metal and grinding of gears.

By the end of 1968, the practice of offering the SCCA Trans-Am-derived cross-ram intake manifolds and tubular headers in the trunk was discontinued. However, you could still purchase those items over the counter at a local Chevy dealership. By adding even more rear end gear ratios (4.10:1, 4.56:1, and 4.88:1) to its option list, Chevrolet enabled those seeking quarter-mile performance to push the envelope without adding more expensive options. The one drawback was driveability on the highways. With the top 4.88 gearset, driving at cruising speed pushed the car near its rpm limits (depending upon which engine was in it), and fuel economy plummeted.

Cosmetically, any Camaro could now be ordered with the ultimate in high-performance styling cues (whether or not there was something under the hood to back up the looks)—the rear spoiler. For the 1967–69 models, the single-piece spoiler rose from the rear decklid, providing the final performance detail for the image-conscious. Shuffling the available paint shades, no fewer than nineteen different colors could be sprayed on the exterior sheetmetal and black or white vinyl top glued to the roof. The SS 396 models received a new hood that featured fake carburetor stacks protruding from two vertical cutouts mounted in the center portion of the hood. A cowl-induction hood was also available as an optional item for the SS and Z28 packages. The SS option 396 big-block also got a boost from engineering with the inclusion of the L89 engine. It was a 375-horse killer that came with aluminum cylinder heads provided by GM's aluminum components supplier, the Winters Foundry, and cut seventy pounds (32kg) of front end weight from the car.

The interior and trim packages remained basically unchanged, except that the upholstery went upscale with the availability of black-and-white checkered houndstooth fabric coverings for the seats. From day one, the dash, instrument cluster, and optional center consoles had taken cues from the latest rage in interior design, the "fighter jet cockpit look." The '68's center console was redesigned and given a more modern appearance. The optional gauge cluster featured rectangular gauges mounted in a "sawtooth" arrangement instead of, as previously, round ones.

By the end of its second year, the Camaro had proven to the automotive world that it wasn't a one-shot wonder. Its highly rated handling and road-holding abilities had quickly earned it the nickname the Hugger. The already strong introductory production and sales totals climbed by some ten thousand units, pushing the production totals even closer to the quarter-million mark.

PAGES 26–27: Sporting "Pro Street" modifications, which were all the rage in the late '80s through the '90s, this '69 Z/28 would make purists cringe!

1969: The Year of Z-Beast

By 1969 America was a nation facing a personal crisis, split between young and old, flower power and those who saw only in red, white, and blue. The "conflict" in Vietnam was in full swing, and the headline events of 1968 had divided the nation's youth. Automakers were not unaware of what was going on in the heartland, either.

Playing off the hippie generation had to be profitable, or so some of the Big Three thought. Chrysler, already into gimmickry a year earlier with the Road Runner, a musclecar with a name copped from the cartoon bird, added the Superbee to its line. Cartoon characters weren't the only game, though. The three divisions of Mopar were offering everything including hot, near-neon-intensity paints, wild striping patterns, and, at one point, the Mod Top, a paisley-patterned vinyl top. Ford, though not into the "hip" look as deeply, did play off the cartoon image with its Cobra and King Cobra lines, and did have some pretty bright colors on the option sheet.

Chevrolet and the Camaro? They didn't need to hit the flower power pocketbooks. The Camaro's prowess had already been proven on racetracks and streets across the country. All GM had to do to keep up was add one set of badges—Z/28. Of course, the Z28 option had been there all along, but now drivers could proclaim it boldly on the street without having to pop the hood to prove it.

Slipping inside a 1969 Camaro, you got the feeling that you were in something much more than a ground-bound machine, more so than in the prior year's models. The round look was gone, replaced with square pods for the gauges and a vertically mounted rectangular climate-control system. The 1968 optional cluster, which had already been given the rectangular treatment, was kept, as it fit right in with the new instrument panel. Ignition was no longer a reach-for-the-dash affair; the switch was moved to a more ergonomic position on the steering column.

It was when you viewed it from the outside that you could tell the stylists had been hard at work, building on the ponycar theme. The rear quarter panels protruded farther from the bodylines, allowing wider tires to fit inside the wheelwells. Those too had changed, taking a flattened appearance at the top, a departure from the constant-radius openings of the past two years. A set of vertical louvers ahead of the rear wheels, while nonfunctional, added a road-racing touch. The soft flowing curve of the body side was given a distinct flank line that started just above the wheel opening in the front fender and carried all the way back to just above the chrome bumper at the tail.

At the nose, the Camaro's grille became a true "eggcrate" style with larger rectangular openings. It also featured a more prominent peak at the center with steeper angles as it split toward the headlights. The Rally Sport nose took on a dramatic look, as the headlight covers now featured three slits, allowing the driver to operate in "stealth mode" at night with reduced illumination, or with the doors opened and full lighting hitting the highway. Can you imagine such an offering in today's highly regulated, safety-conscious industry? For 1969 alone, headlight washers also were an automatic with the Rally Sport package and could be ordered on any other version as well. For the first time, Chevrolet's paint department offered six different two-tone paint combinations, for which fewer than six thousand customers out of more than 240,000 put down the extra $31 and change.

Mechanically, four-wheel power disc brakes featuring four-piston calipers were finally added to the option list, giving drivers the ability to more safely reign in the power they'd put under the hood. Surprisingly, only 206 buyers ponied up the extra cash for this option, code JL8. Steering was also improved, with a variable-ratio system that caused the wheels to turn at a higher rate as the car went deeper into the turn.

For the Z/28, the 302-cubic-inch mill was still the hot ticket. Over the past three years, various magazines had reported quarter-mile times ranging from the high 14s to high 13s, depending on just how each car was optioned and geared, times that left most of its competitors in the dust. Adding to the image, one could option a Z/28 with a cowl-induction hood to take advantage of the high-pressure air

Like it or not, no matter what angle it's viewed from one has to admit that a Pro Street Camaro is one bold brute of a machine.

This Cortez Silver '69, another of the ZL-1s, is in bare-bones stripper form. Note the body color rims and lack of exterior callouts. Definitely not something to mess with on the street or strip!

feed at the base of the windshield and add the rear spoiler, a low bolt-on piece that spanned the width of the rear end.

Ads of the day touted the Z/28 as the "closest thing to a Corvette yet." Other full-page marketing shots played on the reception the Camaro had received from both the automotive press and its readers. One ad, with a headline stating "A word or two to the competition: You lose," noted that the Camaro was the 1969 Reader's Choice in *Car and Driver*.

This was also the final year that the engine option list would be nearly as long as your arm. And by taking advantage of a system that bypassed the regular car-ordering channels within GM, one could get a Camaro with yet another engine package, the 427-cube big-block, the same basic mill that had helped create some of the killer Corvette Sting Ray terrors of the mid- to late '60s. These Camaros, known as COPOs (based on the Central Office Production Order process required to get one), are among the most desirable of all collectible Camaros. This unique buying system, as well as the street scorchers that were created by it, will be discussed in detail in chapter 3.

After the model year 1969 was finished, it would have been easy for GM and Chevrolet executives to sit back and bask in the success that had so quickly come to pass. More than 243,000 Camaros had been sold in '69, the highest production total for the first-generation Chevy F-body. One reason for that high total, though, was that sales were actually a bit sluggish. So, instead of saddling dealerships with leftover 1969 Camaros on the lots when the 1970 models came out, Chevrolet delayed the release of the new car. A September introduction had been the typical practice, but the '70 models didn't come out until the end of February 1970, leading to the existence of 1969 Camaros labeled as 1970 models. Most purists refer to the 1970 F-cars (the situation was the same with Pontiac's Firebird/Trans Am) as 1970$^{1}/_{2}$ models.

Looking back, even by today's standards, the styling of the first iteration of the Camaro doesn't look antiquated and can hold its own, garnering more than a simple glance from most onlookers when out on the roads. With the passing of the decade, the ponycar wars were by no means over. To keep up with the other two of the Big Three, Chevrolet had to keep the Camaro fresh. This time, design and styling weren't as rushed as they were with the first generation, and even better things lay in store.

Coming of Age

The Second–Generation Camaro Carries the Flame

The 1970s heralded a new era, one that still hadn't shed the culturally divisive images of the '60s as much as would have been hoped but one that held new promise for the nation. Though Vietnam, protests, and counterculture idealism would continue to shape the country through the decade, the tradition of musclecars and ponycars faded away faster than anyone would have imagined.

The second evolution of the F-body platform, while similar structurally to the first, would become a better car through refinement and utilization of its front subframe-based design. The initial design phases of the second-generation F-car began as far back as 1966, a longer lead time that allowed further refinement to help an already agile ponycar.

The European look was in vogue, and it showed in the newly styled Camaro that debuted in late 1970. Rather than the front headlamps being set into the grille, the nose now featured a grille narrower than the width of the hood, with the headlights mounted at the front of the rounded fenders. This change resulted in a look highly reminiscent of Ferrari's mid-'60s Lusso. Parking lamps shone from the front valance between the headlamps, and the grille still carried the trademark Camaro angularity. But this year, the nose protruded dramatically instead of maintaining a parallel line like the leading edge of the hood, such as that on the first generation. The windshield rake was also revised, taking an even lower angle to accent the long-nosed styling.

At the tail, the rectangular brake light and turn signal clusters were replaced by four individual round lights, again an image that can be traced to the European flavor the stylists were leaning toward. Vying to be the most visible change with the front-end design was the fastback roofline the new car had adopted. The Camaro wore it well. Its low stance and long nose, combined with the gently raked line at the rear of the car, made it look even more fluid than it had in previous years.

Overall, the Camaro had grown in all directions except up. The car now sat closer to the ground, its height reduced by an inch. The body also developed a beefier tone by going from 72.5 to 74.4 inches (184 to 189cm) in width. Though the wheelbase remained the same at 108 inches (274cm), the overall length increased from 184.7 to 186.7 inches (469 to 474cm). Safety and crash-impact standards were becoming key elements in design, and the Camaro now sported a set of side-impact beams in the doors for the first time. Inside, the dash surfaces also played to the safety-conscious by having less protrusive angles. The square gauge pods disappeared, replaced by two main round gauges surrounded by smaller ancillary gauges set in a wide cluster centered directly in front of the driver. Optional instrumentation was no longer console-mounted but was moved to the main instrument panel. For open-air enthusiasts, there was no droptop offering. The next time a convertible roof would appear as a Camaro option would be in 1987.

OPPOSITE: Extensively restyled for 1970, the second-generation Camaro's front-end design could ironically be traced directly to Ford's Allegro II sports car prototype of the mid-1960s.

By 1970, the optional SS engine lineup had been pared down to two versions of the 396 big-block: the L34 option, which put out 350 horsepower, and the top-dog 375 horsepower L78. The base SS mill was a 350-cube small-block rated at 300 horsepower.

OPPOSITE: Showing its owner's taste for a personalized ride, this '70 sports a non-factory sunroof. With convertibles out of the lineup until the third generation, this was as close to open- air cruising as one could get.

Handling was improved, with revised spring and shock rates both front and rear, helping the Hugger stay true to its moniker. New bushings in the rear multileaf springs helped ride attributes. No matter how similar, though, first- and second-generation front suspension and subframe systems will not cross over. Because the subframe was widened where it attached at the front of the body, the car sat lower and offered reduced body roll through a lower center of gravity. The steering linkage, which before had connected to the steering box behind the center of the front wheels, was moved ahead of the wheel's centerline, providing a more forgiving cornering characteristic when put into a turn a little bit too hot.

The little 327 was no longer an SS option and, as with the '69 model, the base V8 was the 307-cubic-incher. When it came to the Z/28 package, its racing derivation followed course with what was actually happening on the tracks. For the Trans-Am series, the SCCA upped the allowable dis-

Early first-generation Rally Sports optioned with the SS or Z/28 packages lost the RS badging but still could be identified by a number of features, including the inboard parking lights, body-color door handle inserts, and distinct grille.

placement levels, so racing Camaros were allowed to use the venerable 350-cubic-incher. Homologation was still a requirement, a fact that resulted in the Z/28 option having a 360-hp 350-cube power plant. The high-winding 302 mill also disappeared from the option sheet, but it wasn't a bad loss. The new LT-1 350 featured four-bolt main caps, a high-rise aluminum intake manifold, and carburetion via a four-barrel Rochester Quadrajet. The biggest of the Chevy big-blocks, the 454, came very close to being offered as a regular production option. But close doesn't count in this business. For the first time, the Z/28's hi-po power plant could be coupled with an automatic transmission, in this case the Turbo Hydromatic 400. The 396 power plant was modified, the new LS-3, as it was coded, offering a few more cubic inches than before. These versions are often referred to as either 400- or 402-cubic-inchers, depending on the source.

In addition to the extensive sheetmetal revisions, the cosmetic packaging also changed in 1970. Color offerings returned to single-tone finishes, and only fifteen different paints were offered; to the surprise of many enthusiasts, not a single shade of black was available. Though one could still combine the RS and SS options as well as the RS and Z/28 options, when done, the RS badging was not included. At the tail, the original spoiler that mated to the trunk could be had, but a new spoiler was available as a COPO option for any model. It featured wraparound end caps that carried the spoiler's angled plane slightly down the side of the quarter panels. Two years later, this radical-looking piece, developed jointly between Pontiac and Chevrolet, would become standard issue.

As for hinting at things to come, the 1970 Camaro sales showed that, by the end of the 1970 production run, just under 125,000 Camaros had been built, despite the rave reviews it had received. Though it may seem like a massive drop from the prior year's production totals, you must remember that the late introduction of the model coupled with the long production run of the prior year had certainly

This '70 RS Z/28 sports the famed factory Rally wheels, a defining option on any Camaro. Low-back buckets with headrests would bow out the

OPPOSITE: Based on the SCCA's decision to increase allowable engine displacement for the 1970 Trans-Am racing series, the Z/28 Camaros sported 360 horsepower 350-cubic-inch engines.

Extensively restyled for 1970, this Z/28 Camaro sports the full-width chrome bumper that was standard issue, rather than the split bumper of the RS package, shown on page 37.

had a measurable impact. Adding to the low totals of the long '69 run was a United Auto Workers (UAW) strike late in the year that stranded the assembly lines for more than two months. Far worse lay ahead.

1971: The Hi-Po Hiatus Begins

By the early 1970s, the war in Vietnam wasn't the only source of protest in the country. The environment became a rallying point for activists, and the industrial manufacturing industry came under fire, for both the pollution its methods of manufacturing produced and the pollution coming from its products. The fact that high-performance street machines posed an inherent risk to motorists' lives wasn't lost on the insurance industry, either, and insurance rates not only began to reflect the insured's driving record but also became based on what he had under the hood. With that kind of public pressure, the EPA started to keep a close eye on what was coming from Detroit.

What upset motorheads the most, however, was the apparent plummeting of horsepower levels. Though power output did drop slightly industry-wide (most manufacturers had been deliberately underrating advertised horsepower for years), this was because the industry had

The SS 396 emblem was more pronounced than in previous years, highlighting the image-conscious thinking of upper management.

PAGES 40–41: Now a bona fide appearance and performance package, the Z/28 Camaro didn't sell quite as well as in '68–'69, but it still made up nearly 9,000 of the more than 100,000 Camaros sold in 1970.

begun to list net horsepower and torque levels instead of the traditional gross power ratings most enthusiasts were accustomed to. The difference was that the net listing took into account the losses from the driveline and accessories, whereas the gross ratings had always shown an engine's output with nothing attached.

Coinciding with the change in power rating, the previous year both the 396 and the 350 had been built with 10.25 and 11.0:1 compression levels. This year, the highest compression being pumped out by these Chevy engines was 9.0:1, in the Z/28. This drop in compression levels corresponded with an edict from the very top of GM's corporate structure that dictated that all GM engines withstand the reduced-octane, lower-lead fuels that were beginning to flow through the pumps. Though 8.5:1 compression was the order, the hi-po engines were allowed to go slightly higher, hence the Z/28's rating one-half point above the rest. Another engine, a high-winding small-block capable of moving 400 cubic inches of air through its cylinders, was planned, designed, and canceled, just like the 454 had been a year earlier.

If the sheer power of the ponycars wasn't attracting buyers anymore, then the styling would have to play a more important role. To that end, the '71s took on more luxurious appointments. The standard badging boasted a new scripted styling. A dozen new colors came out, along with an additional choice for those who wanted the upscale look of a vinyl top. Wheel covers, always an important styling accessory, were revised. With the new optional three-piece rear spoiler came a front air dam that was a carryover from SCCA racing and was standard issue with the Z/28.

Inside, high-back bucket seats were lifted from the Vega and proved to be quite popular. The soft surface work that had started the year before by eliminating many protruding angles in the dash continued with new padded coverings, which reduced the chance for injuries on impact.

Though the fears of the enthusiasts hadn't yet been realized, some ten thousand fewer units sold, and it was only a matter of time before the roots of those fears became reality.

1972: The UAW Makes Matters Worse

There was a time when one of the best-selling, best-handling passenger cars ever developed in this nation nearly met an untimely demise. In 1972, F-body production was reduced solely to the line at the Norwood, Ohio, facility. When the UAW struck again in April, as it had in late '69, the F-body's fate came closer to death than it ever had or would.

For four months, the line was idle and Camaros and Firebirds gathered dust, never fully completed. By the time negotiators for the General and the UAW reached an agreement, the new 1973 safety standards were requirements that the cars would have to meet, and what was half-complete on the line wouldn't meet them. Therefore, more than 2,000 incomplete F-cars, both Pontiac and Chevrolet, were taken to the crusher. Only 68,651 Camaros made it into buyers' hands in 1972; such low production totals wouldn't be seen again until the 1990s.

Not only did the strike hurt production, it made GM uneasy, and talk soon circulated that the Camaro and its sister, the Firebird, would not be around the following year. Credit is most often given to Alex Mair, Chevy's engineering head, and Bill Collins, Pontiac's assistant chief engineer, for saving the F-body. The rumors were true, and it took formal, face-to-face presentations in front of the decision-making committees before it was decided to save the platform.

What *did* make it into the hands of the motoring public was a Camaro that had been continuing along the lines of the image- and safety-enhanced route. Simple touches like map pockets and coin trays added to the door panels were among the convenience-oriented details that buyers were beginning to deem important. The first of the single-system lap and shoulder harnesses was also implemented. In prior years, separate belts had held drivers and passengers in place. Another change likely executed because of safety and insurance concerns was a new floor shifter for the standard gearbox, which prevented accidental shifts into reverse through a pushdown lock button.

By 1971, power levels were based on net instead of gross ratings. This upset owners, who thought that performance had disappeared overnight. This '71 Tuxedo Black Z/28 came with a 330-horse rating and lower compression levels that dropped the power rating a bit, but in reality the seemingly much lower power levels weren't far off from those of previous models.

This '71 Z/28 displays good looks and muscle with restyled Rally wheels painted in body-matching Antique White.

The Super Sport option now left buyers with only two choices: a 200-hp (net) 350 or the 240-hp (net) Turbo Fire LS-3. The LS-3 big-block wasn't available to California buyers because it didn't pass that state's emissions standards. The Z/28 package lost its spoiler as standard issue, and it now had to be purchased as an optional item.

1973: The Year of the Trade-Off

It was now official: "high-performance" was a dirty phrase, and the growing distance from the days of hi-po street terrors was rapidly becoming a chasm. The first victim of this new product approach from Chevy was the killer LS-3 engine of the Super Sport option. In its place, Chevrolet debuted the Type LT, but not as an option. No, this new offering—its name an abbreviation of Luxury Touring—was an entirely separate model from the Camaro line. The Type LT hid a detuned Turbo Fire 350 under the hood. In this version, it put out 20 hps less than 1973's weakest 350 had generated. The Type LT also came with power steering and the interior decor and quiet sound option package as standard equipment, and it stickered nearly $400 more than a base V8 Sport Coupe.

If enthusiasts bemoaned the loss of the SS, then they could at least take comfort in the fact that the Z/28 was still

around. Again, the powerplants were watered down; the Z/28's L-82 350, though still a four-bolt main block, like its predecessor, lost 10 hps to the previous LT-1 350. Part of that loss can be attributed to the low-rise cast-iron intake manifold and smog-equipment-shod Holley four-barrel carburetor mounted atop it. The Z/28's powerplant now used hydraulic lifters, and in that regard the '73 350 was an improvement despite the power loss, since one didn't have to spend every other weekend readjusting the valve lash, a typical requirement with the earlier solid-lifter engine.

This change also led to more comfort, with optional air-conditioning available in the Z/28 for the first time. Production costs dropped because of the new engine, and the savings were passed on to the buyer. In '72, the Z/28 option in a Sport Coupe was $769; in '73 it went down to $598, $502 if added to the Type LT. Because of tougher collision-impact requirements, the small "bumperettes" of the RS package were mounted on stronger isolators and beefier brackets, providing better impact absorption. But to get those, you had to be quick about it. After the first of the year, all orders got the full-width bumper treatment. The RS's unique look, so well known out on the road, made its final appearance as a stylistically independent Camaro. When it returned a year and a half later, it shared the same grille and headlamp design as the other Camaros.

The Camaro's front-end styling continued along much the same lines that it had since the second-generation plat-

In 1972, the last of the RPO Z27 Super Sports had rolled off the assembly line, taking with them the final big-blocks. This '73 Z/28 represents the best bang for the buck with its 350-cube small-block.

form was designed, as did the rest of the body's sheetmetal. It was the creature comforts that received the lion's share of attention this year. Power windows, controlled with two-way switches mounted on the console, were available for the first time. One much-beloved option, though, bit the dust. The "stirrup"-style floor-mounted automatic transmission shifter was replaced with a more typical stick-and-knob piece, and the optional center console was redesigned. By the end of the year, production totals had rebounded from the dismal numbers of '72. More than 96,000 buyers drove off in new Camaros that year, and the Type LT was something of which the folks at Chevy could be proud. Nearly one-third of all sales were of the new model, whereas a year before, fewer than ten thousand SS packages had been ordered. Maybe marketing was right: image was something to be reckoned with, even more so than performance. In the following years, GM would put performance on the back burner and cater to those seeking looks with attitude.

The legendary Hurst stick-and-ball shifter mated to a four-speed gearbox. For gearheads, life just didn't get any better than this.

The COPO Collusion

Chevrolet Arms the Everyday Joe with a 427–Cubic-Inch Rocket

It started officially in 1969. Defying GM's front office, which had imposed a ban on placing engines larger than 400 cubic inches in passenger cars, there came to be known a system by which you could order and purchase — if you had enough money, knowledge, and clout — one of the vehicles that have become known as the ultimate Camaros, the COPOs. An acronym for Central Office Production Order, a COPO was the only way you could get the factory to install a 427-cubic-inch big-block in the Camaro. And it wasn't as if you could stop by and check off an option box at your local dealership. For a COPO order to go through, Chevy's Central Office and its engineering department had to give the okay. And COPO wasn't solely for engine packages; it could also be used to pick up other performance- or appearance-enhancing parts for the Camaro, like the COPO 9796 three-piece spoiler (1970).

Prior to this process, the 427 had been available only in the Corvette. Had the engine line available in the Corvette been allowed as a part of the Camaro option list, it is likely that Chevrolet would have had on its hands a car capable of outperforming the Vette, a situation that absolutely could not be allowed. The most common of the COPO packages was COPO 9561, the cast-iron (L-72) version of the 427. No exact production number is known, but upward of five hundred COPO 9561 Camaros were reportedly built, according to various sources. The advertised power output of the cast-

iron 427 was on par with Chrysler's 426 street Hemi, 425 horsepower. In other words, it was underrated by far. COPO 9737 added a 140-mph (224km) speedometer

COPO 9560 created one of the most absolutely outrageous Camaros ever built, the order equipping one's Camaro with the all-aluminum-block ZL-1 427. The plan had been to top these behemoths with 850-cfm Holley carburetors, which would have provided enough fuel to lend credibility to the term "sewer-sized" carburetors. In actuality, very few of the COPO 9560 Camaros were built with these huge four-barrels. Holley simply could not provide enough of them to meet the demand. Unlike most of the SS engine options, the COPOs didn't set you back just a few hundred dollars. No, these gouged deep into the bank account, with the top-dog ZL-1 adding more than $4,000 to the cost of the Camaro—that's for a car with a base price just under three grand! Both the cast-iron and aluminum 427s came with the ZL2 cowl-induction hood that was also an option for the SSes and Z/28s.

Of course, the ZL-1s were built for one reason: to put Chevy back on top of the drag racing winners list. Some sixty-nine were built, fifty to meet the National Hot Rod Association's (NHRA) production requirement and an additional nineteen that went to a select few with enormous clout. Based on an aluminum block with steel cylinder sleeves and aluminum cylinders (all cast at the Winters Foundry), the ZL-1s were derived directly from the Corvette,

OPPOSITE: With its stock SS option striping, the only giveaway that one is facing a '67 427-powered Nickey Camaro is a diminutive set of emblems that went along with the conversions offered through Nickey Chevrolet in Chicago and Bill Thomas's dealerships on the East and West Coasts.

OPPOSITE: In 1986, two 427 iron-block Yenko Super Car Camaros squared off at the staging lights of Englishtown, New Jersey's Raceway Park for *MuscleCars* magazine. The results? Driven by the owners, the tire-smoking YSCs clicked off 13.15 at 112.92 mph (181.69kph) (four-speed) and 13.05 at 105.50 mph (169.75kph) (automatic).

Don Yenko initially started out doing 427 swaps through his Canonsburg, Pennsylvania, dealership. In '68 he found the COPO process made life much simpler by allowing factory-built 427 Camaros to arrive, where they were given striping and other buyer-requested options as part of his Yenko Super Car package. Little did the buyer know that Yenko didn't install the 427s in the later YSCs.

in which they had been offered as a regular production option. (Two Corvette ZL-1s are known to have been ordered and built and are of inestimable value.) The goal of these particular machines? Domination on the drag strips in one of the most fiercely contested categories of the day: Super Stock. Whereas Pro Stock now reigns supreme in the NHRA, Super Stock (supposedly a class in which cars that were somewhat available to the public were raced) was the corporate attention-getter in the late '60s and early '70s. It all went back to that line: Win on Sunday, Sell on Monday ... If drag racing fans saw the Camaro romping on the Fords and Chryslers, they just might change their minds about buying a Blue Oval or Mopar and head over to their nearest Chevrolet dealer.

Super Tuner Street Terrors

At the same time speed freaks were catching on to the COPO deal, a select number of tuners and dealers came to the realization that not only could they create the cars of enthusiasts' dreams, but the very same cars would go a long way toward making their names known in the aftermarket circles. And so were born Camaros of special distinction, those that today are among the most highly prized collectibles.

In New York, Joel Rosen of Motion Performance, an aftermarket speed shop, and Baldwin Chevrolet teamed up and offered g-force junkies the Baldwin Motion Camaros.

Like the Camaro on the previous page, this Baldwin Motion ride is a '69. If the Daytona Yellow wasn't enough to catch your eye, the jacked-up stance and 427 badging surely would.

Inside a Nickey Camaro, just like on the outside, there was little to let one know what lurked under the hood.

This line soon expanded through the COPO process to include Corvettes and Chevelles, all bearing different levels of tweaking through Baldwin Motion's Phase III packages. Baldwin Motion had jumped into the game almost from day one of the Camaro, offering SS 427 Camaro conversions. By 1969, the Phase II and III Baldwin Motion Camaros were the King Kongs of the street. These highly modified Camaros (they weren't just lightly worked COPOs) could come with not only the 427 but also the top-production big-block from Chevrolet, the 454. If you had an unlimited bank account at your disposal, you could really go to town with Motion's catalog: Super Bite traction bar suspension, big-block Corvette-style hoods, even full factory warranties for noncompetition-only engines could be had, and, in most cases, with GMAC financing!

Unlike most of the other converters, Baldwin Motion kept at it into the early 1970s, until the federal government stepped in (in 1974) with what amounted to a cease and desist order. Despite that, the overseas market was still sellable, and BM 454 Camaros were exported until late 1975.

Nestled in the rolling hills of Pennsylvania was another Chevrolet dealership whose name would become fabled in the world of the F-car: Don Yenko. Yenko took the same route as Motion Performance with the Camaro, not only

PAGES 50–51: The absolute heavyweights of the tuner Camaros were built by the New York–based combined effort known as Baldwin Motion, a shop that liked to stuff 454-cubic-inch big-blocks under the hoods. In the background is a Baldwin Motion Corvette. All you needed was the cash, and GMAC financing was available!

In a defining moment of history, Don Yenko (right) and noted tuner Dickie Harrell set the Super Stock drag racing world on its ear. On April 21, 1969, driver Ed Hendrick put his foot to work and sent one of Yenko's 427-powered Camaros down the drag strip in York, Pennsylvania, on an 11.94 at a 114.5 mph (184.23kph) run. That was with Goodyear 8-inch-wide (20.5cm) slicks and a set of headers. Said Hendrick, "I'm sure we could have gone a lot faster but the clutch was so rough I couldn't make any power shifts. They could have given me a lot better prepared car."

stylizing his cars with otherworldly levels of horsepower and torque, but adding visual cues to make it clearly known that the wailing roar that had just passed you in a blur of color and earthshaking vibrations was none other than one of his babies, a Yenko Super Car.

He'd started out in 1965 with Corvairs, eventually building a Stinger Corvair that took home an SCCA National Championship. When the Camaro came out in 1967, it was a given that it would be a Yenko Super Car. For the most part, the Yenko Super Car Camaros were based on COPO 9561 and were given the stripe and 427 badge treatment. For options, Yenko offered a Stewart-Warner gauge cluster and 8,000-rpm tachometer and Doug Thorley headers, and

automatics that came from Chevrolet could be given Hurst dual-gate shifters. By the time one was done, an 11-second ET in the quarter-mile was an easy task. In the early 1980s, Yenko waved his wand over the Camaro again, creating the Turbo Z, a 13-second-capable machine powered by a turbocharged 350.

The East Coast folks weren't the only ones having fun, though. Nickey Chevrolet in Chicago offered a 427 Camaro package that usually started out as an SS 350 Camaro. Nickey also offered its conversions through Bill Thomas's Chevrolet franchises on both the East and West Coasts. Thomas had made his name designing, among other things, performance header systems. The Nickey Camaros

Looking sinister in basic black, this '69 Yenko could deliver pulse-pounding performance that would make the blood run cold in any Mopar or Blue Oval challenger.

Command Central in a Yenko Camaro was a pretty spartan affair. His package included the 8,000-rpm tachometer shown to the right of the steering wheel, and a 140-mph (225kph) speedometer in place of the regular production unit.

No matter what angle it's viewed from, a Camaro shows the stance that earned it the nickname "the Hugger." When it was a 1969 Yenko SC with a COPO 9651 427 cubic inch big block under the hood, you knew it was a Hugger with a bellacious heartbeat.

Though this 427 has obviously been restored to its period-correct "stock" status, you can bet one of the first things to go on this mighty mill was the air pump in front of the air filter and any other smog-related equipment.

were a bit more subtle in appearance than the Yenko and Baldwin Motion Camaros. There were no unique stripe and graphics packages added to the Nickey cars, just an identification badge on the fenders. Basically these creations catered to those seeking the sleeper look with wide-awake acceleration.

Of the specialty Camaro packages, perhaps some of the least known are those that came from the garage of Dana Chevrolet in Southgate, California. It isn't because they were any less the ultimate street machines, though; it's just that fewer were made and fewer survive today than any of the

others. The Stage I Dana 427 Camaros were home to the L-72 cast-iron big-block, SS trim package, four-speed gearbox, and heavy-duty cooling system. A Stage II package added a revised suspension system that was still streetable but offered better performance on the drag strip. The Stage III Dana took that one step further with an all-out race suspension and other on-track-only goodies.

There was also a number of even lesser known dealerships that did 427 and 454 conversions, most of which worked with fewer than fifty Camaros in the late '60s. In the world of today's Camaros, the good times have started to

When Nickey Chevrolet in Chicago installed the 427, they set it back in the compartment just enough to provide the perfect weight distribution over the front spindles for improved launches and slightly better road handling. The emblem below was about the only visual clue as to what motivated this '67 Camaro.

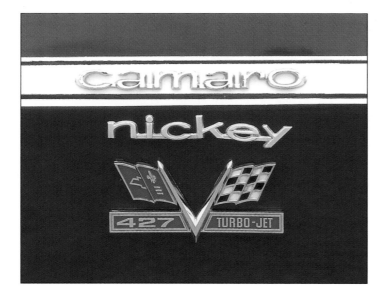

roll again. Not only does the aftermarket offer plenty of goodies for the LT-1 and LS-1 small-block 350s, outfits like Callaway Competition, Doug Rippie Motorsports, RK Sport, Lingenfelter Performance Engineering, SLP Engineering, and others will turn your street-legal Camaro into a road-going cruise missile capable of hanging with the best conversions of yesteryear.

Dana Chevrolet produced a limited number of 427 Dana Camaros. This Hugger Orange '68 began life as an SS 350 and received the uniquely ducted hood, 425-horse 427, heavy duty suspension and radiator, and a four-speed gearbox, among other items.

Big Brother Is Watching

The Industry Bows to a New Master, as Performance Becomes a Dirty Word

4

As the gradually creeping regulations of both safety and fuel efficiency began to make their mark on the automotive industry, enthusiasts saw a direct impact on the performance of their favorite ponycar. The decisions of a group of countries in the Middle East in late 1973 had dire and far-reaching effects on the high-performance automotive industry. The consortium of oil-producing countries known by the acronym OPEC (Organization of the Petroleum Exporting Countries) saw fit to block the sale of crude oil, creating a contrived-for-profit oil crisis. With prices skyrocketing at the pumps, the entire circle of leadfoots who had gained pleasure from the ability to hop into a street machine at a moment's notice now had to carefully regulate their right feet. Long lines at the pumps became common, as did the practice of distributing the lifeblood of the car based on the final digit on its license plate.

Not only did the oil embargo hit those who owned musclecars, it put a major dent in the Big Three's ponycar and musclecar programs. Though never as highly profitable as more sedate grocery-getter car lines, the hi-po machines afforded manufacturers the ultimate in visibility — i.e., free advertising where it mattered, on the everyday roads of the country. Soon, weekly cruise-in spots were deserted. High-horsepower cars were a dime a dozen in the classifieds, and those looking to get out of the V8 rear-wheel-drive gas-guzzler hobby usually took a huge hit in the wallet in order to get themselves into a newly emerging economy-designed commuter car.

Without outright ending F-car production, Chevrolet was left with only one option: forsake the high-performance heritage and continue to market the Camaro based on its fast, fluid looks. Not only would looks be important but so would luxury, the addition of which came with its own exacting toll: weight to overload an already slowing thoroughbred in midstride.

The 1974 Camaro engine lineup did not change from the previous year. The Z/28 option still included the 245-hp 350-cubic-inch V8, and the Type LT was powered by a detuned version of the 350. GM also introduced its High Energy Ignition system (HEI), which eliminated the points-style ignition and the associated points-replacement maintenance hassle. Some of the safety standards now being set required extensive redesigns, particularly in the area of impact absorption. The stylists incorporated a new front bumper system into a "shovel-nose" treatment at the front of the '74 Camaro, which would define the Camaro look all the way through the 1980s. After 1974, the Z/28 option would take a vacation, reappearing as a separate model in 1977. Power-hungry Camaro lovers were forced to face reality in 1975. Gone was the Z/28, joining the ranks of retired hi-po options like the SS.

But Chevrolet and its pony weren't the only ones making concessions. Plymouth and Dodge pulled their E-bodied

As a sort of token offering to the power hungry, the 1980 Z28s came with a 190-horsepower 350 that featured a quasi-cowl-induction hood scoop with a flap that opened when the accelerator was floored to let outside air in.

The Camaro was the mainstay race car of the International Race of Champions series from 1975 to 1990 and gave the public a direct link to a product that they could watch racing on television. In the 1980s Chevrolet would cash in on that by offering the IROC Zs.

'Cuda and Challenger lines altogether. Ford turned the Mustang — which had left its Falcon roots and evolved into the fastback-styled Boss 302s and Mach I, II, and III coupes of the late '60s and early '70s — into a complete econobox. The Mustang II debuted in 1974 as a near subcompact like the Pinto and sporting choices for only a four- or six-cylinder engine. This was the ponycar competition, the car that started it all? It truly was a sad day for fans of the Blue Oval!

The most visible change to the Camaro was at the rear, where a new wraparound rear window was finally incorporated. Always a safety concern, the earlier Camaros had been known for having poor rearward visibility because of their large roof support pillar. Though the wraparound window had been on the design table for several years, fitment

problems and leaks prevented its introduction until the 1975 model year. For looks, Chevrolet brought back the Rally Sport option. This time around, it had become more cosmetic than ever before, featuring an all-out blackout treatment combined with a new tricolor pinstriping scheme. Always known for its dynamic front-end treatment, this latest RS package was not unique in that regard.

America celebrated its bicentennial in 1976 with massive fireworks displays, tall ships sailing, and just about anything commemorative that could be printed, stamped, or engraved. However, gearheads, unless they still harbored something in the garage from a few years back, could find few fireworks with which to celebrate. A new V8 was in the works for the base models, but this 140-hp 305-cubic-inch

power plant was nothing to get excited about. The top performer was still the 350 small-block, now eking out a paltry 165 horsepower. Surprisingly, though, demand was still strong and some 180,000 new-car buyers elected to take home a Camaro. The Type LT soldiered on as the top-of-the-line model. Performance improvements included power brakes for all V8-equipped F-cars and cruise control.

1977–81: The Z Sets the Standard

The Z/28 was back as an entity unto itself, and it offered a glimmer of hope. Not only did it have the racy styling that had come to be associated with speed, but its performance took a turn for the better with the 350-cube V8. Now putting out 185 horsepower, the 350-cube mill would be the mainstay Camaro engine, eventually cranking out 190 horsepower in the 1980–81 Z28s, until it was discontinued with the emergence of the third-generation Camaro in 1982.

The new Z featured front and rear spoilers that reflected the model's previous famed history, as well as bold graphics on its hood to spell it out. For 1977–81, the Z28 was a standalone model, meaning that it couldn't be combined with the Rally Sport or Type LTs the way earlier versions could. A set of fender louvers that allowed hot air to be ventilated out of the engine compartment was added to the '78 Z28s. The Rally Sports for that year offered a two-tone paint treatment and could be split into two versions, the Rally Sport coupe or the Type LT Rally Sport.

GM's decision to keep the F-car alive proved shrewd, as the two millionth Camaro built rolled off the lines during the spring of 1978. Even though convertible models never became a reality in the second-generation Camaros, the T-top-style roof made a mid-season appearance in 1978. From 1977 to 1979, more than 200,000 Camaros were purchased each year, proving that straightline speed wasn't the only thing that sold ponycars. The successful Type LT bowed out in '79, replaced by the Berlinetta, which, like the Rally Sport,

OPPOSITE: Long after the competition had shied away from performance and either downsized their once sporty ponycars to little econoboxes or eliminated them altogether, Chevrolet and the Camaro soldiered on. For 1980, the Z28 got a functional wide-open throttle activated hood scoop and a 190-hp 350-cubic-inch small-block.

Lovers of the first generation Z/28s generally regard the second generation versions as imposters that are all bark and no bite. Viewed from either end, the 1974 Z28 package was far more striking in appearance than it was in performance.

was considered a separate model. Inside, a revised instrument panel and antitheft steering column greeted the driver. The Z28 soldiered on but lost a bit of its bite, with the 350's net horsepower rating dropping by 10 to 175.

By 1980, the second-generation design was getting a bit long in the tooth. Surprisingly, the Z28 got a fresh infusion of blood, a new rearward-facing hood scoop and other performance tweaks that boosted output to 190 horsepower. The surprising thing about the new scoop was that it was functional. At full throttle, a solenoid opened the ducting, providing fresh cold air for a bit of oomph that had been lacking. The grille was revised with a smaller mesh pattern, giving it more detail.

The Rally Sport model continued on as a paint stripe and rear spoiler treatment. For those still wanting the racy looks but worried about the prices at the pumps, a 120-hp

267-cubic-inch V8, coded L39, was available. This engine wasn't much for the go-fast crowd, but you could still say you had a V8 under the hood!

With 1981 came the passage of the Rally Sport into the history books. The Berlinetta models continued to provide the comfort that the Type LTs had in the past, and the Z/28 continued with no real changes. In its final three years, sales of the second generation of the Hugger had dropped steadily from well over a quarter-million in '79 to 126,000 in '81. After twelve years in production, the second-generation Camaros became a part of Chevrolet history. The design had lasted longer than anyone expected and, despite the loss of performance over the years, had catered to the tastes of its dedicated following quite admirably. The Camaro that Chevrolet had planned for 1982 would have a tough act to follow.

PAGES 68-69: Herb Adams is best known for his work with Pontiac in developing the Trans Am. He raced a street-legal T/A, dubbed the Fire-Am, in the 1979 24 hours at Daytona. He also tinkered with the Chevy version of the F-car. His Cheverra, based on a 1980 Camaro, featured race-level handling and performance mods and was offered through his company, VSE.

In 1979 the Berlinetta arrived as a separate model, replacing the Type LT. It was a model aimed directly at the image- and style-conscious.

Mastering the Machine Age

High Technology Guides the Third-Generation Camaro

5

For its third time around, the Camaro's designers could have followed several lines of thought that were permeating the industry at the time. As a concession to economy, the Camaro could have been transformed into a sporty-looking front-wheel-driver that a true enthusiast wouldn't be caught dead in. It could have continued down its previous path, keeping mild V8s with a rear-wheel-drive arrangement and the racy look. Or it could take a bold, aggressive turn with styling unlike anything previously, and power and handling to match — which is what happened. What appeared in the brochures and on the dealership floors combined a new aggressive styling with the mild manners that had evolved over the years.

Take one look at a 1982–92 Camaro and you'll reach the same conclusion that the designers did: the round look was out. The angular belt line, a trademark of the previous design, was even more pronounced, giving the sports coupe a very squat appearance. The overall bodyline was flat, with just a hint of a forward slope showing on the fenders. The leading edges of the fenders and hood were set flush with the nose, which still wore the slight peak at its center and carried the trademark shovel-nose look that had started in 1974. The roofline likewise was low and devoid of com-

pound angles, with the exception of the back glass. Rearward visibility wouldn't be a problem in this design, as it had a broad expanse of rear glass that served as a hatchback, something no other Camaro had ever had.

The overall image repeated that which the first Camaros had projected: low, sleek, and fast. In this case, it was very aerodynamic and intentionally so. Sporting a drag coefficient of .368, the new Camaro was the most efficient wind-cheating passenger car ever designed and built by GM up to that time. Depending on how it was equipped, the new pony weighed in right around 3,000 pounds (1,360kg), nearly 500 pounds (225kg) lighter than the 1981 version. The length was shortened by just under 10 inches (25cm) to 187.8 (477cm). Because of changing crash-impact standards, the second-generation Camaro's overall length had grown from 188 inches to 197.6 inches by 1978. The wheelbase shrank as well, from 108 to 101 inches (274 to 256.5cm), height was reduced only marginally, and the car's width decreased by 2.8 inches (7cm).

At the rear, although the aging solid-axle rear-end design remained, it was now suspended by coil springs instead of leaf springs. In addition to the coil springs, the rear end was braced against deflection in the corners with a track bar connected to the underbody on the left side, and to the axle on the right. A torque arm was used to limit lateral axle movement (previously associated with the windup of the leaf springs) and bolted onto the top of the center differential, running forward along the driveshaft and attaching to the underside of the body next to the transmission case. These changes resulted in a marked improvement in both handling and ride quality. A front subframe still was incorporated for the front suspension, but it too had been revised. Instead of using upper and lower control arms with springs and shocks, the new design used a MacPherson strut attached to the lower control arm, with the coil spring sandwiched between the lower control arm and subframe. This system also required that the front portion of the body be constructed with a strut tower in a unitized body manner for the first time.

Ralph Kramer, who had started at GM in 1973 and moved to the Chevrolet division in 1979, was still working with design and engineering when the third-generation Camaro was developed. (In 1986, he moved into the public relations department.) He explained what the thought was in the design department in regard to creating a wind-cheating passenger car:

> We did a lot of work on the aerodynamics on that car. We thought that it was the slickest big production car on the road. We had the wind tunnel. GM was very heavy into wind-tunnel testing and had a brand-new one that got used quite a bit. You could argue that working on the aerodynamic drag coefficient for a passenger car is a worthless bit of effort in that nobody goes fast enough to make it worth the difference, but for the Camaro, we did it because we always tried to make it look really swoopy. Of course, the next question with that type of look was, "What's the aerodynamic drag coefficient?" so we tried to back it up with some real engineering that both looked aero and was.

As this latest version of the Camaro was becoming a bit obsolete, Kramer related that it nearly became a front-wheel-drive sports coupe, something that, looking back,

PAGES 76–77: The 1986 Z28s came with a 155-horsepower 305-cubic-inch engine as standard equipment, but two 190-horse versions could be had as well.

Cross-Fire fuel injection debuted as a Z28-only option and provided more power than the computer-controlled carburetor systems in use at the time. It would prove to be a short-lived fuel delivery system that wasn't understood by most enthusiasts who'd been raised on carburetion.

surely would have sounded the car's death knell. At the time, Ford was set to introduce the front-wheel-drive Probe, and word in the industry was that this would replace the Mustang, which by now had evolved from the Mustang II of the mid- to late '70s into the 1979 Mustang based on the Fairmont's Fox chassis.

Kramer said, "In the mid-'80s, the word came through that the Camaro was going to be a front-wheel-drive car. It filtered down that the decision had been made, and that was a very difficult thing for some of us to deal with. Fortunately, we ended up not building a front-wheel-drive Camaro. To the extent that the central office staff was always over at design staff, you had the big debate over whether the car should be front-wheel drive. I think the sentiment at Chevy in the late '80s, which was about the time that design work had started on the fourth generation, was that it had to be rear-wheel drive or it just wouldn't be a

Camaro. You could call it something else and make it perform and be a good seller, but if it was to be a Camaro, it had to be rear-wheel drive. That issue delayed the design of the next version of the car; the struggle to resolve that issue took so much time that the new Camaro came out late."

From 1982 to 1986, the Camaro was burdened with a 305-cubic-inch V8, coded the LG4. Featuring throttle-body fuel injection (TBI), this small-block wasn't known for its neck-snapping acceleration. The Z28 tradition continued in the new model, equipped with distinctive five-spoke alloy wheel, and, among other amenities, an optional version of the 305 with a short-lived fuel system known as Cross-Fire injection that boosted horsepower from the standard version's 145 to 165. Not exactly boasting a staggering output level, this Z28 option could be ordered only with an automatic transmission. In 1982–83, the Z28 went further with the weight reduction by including a fiberglass hood. The Z's

Open or

The year 1984 may not have ushered in a completely Orwellian world, but the government still managed to have its say, requiring the Central High Mount Stop Lamp (CHMSL) in 1986. GM countered with advances in engine management that meant more power without violating EPA emissions interior also brought the driver additional comfort in the form of special LearSiegler Conteur seats, six-way adjustable buckets that at the time were considered the best that could be found in a production passenger car. The '83 Camaro saw the introduction of an optional five-speed gearbox that came as standard equipment in both the Berlinetta and Z28. The '83 Z28 also got a boost from an offering called the High Output (HO) version of the 305, which upped the power ante by 10 horsepower.

The Berlinetta versions also continued until the 1986 model year. Whereas Ford had inadvertently tapped into the female buyer's market with the Mustang from day one, Chevrolet would have to wage an advertising campaign to lure in sales in the "secretary" market. Said Kramer:

The Camaro was always a car that we had to work at in order to make it appeal to young women. We had the Berlinetta and several other factory versions well done up, but with not as much power. We always had the insurance and emissions issues to deal with. The 305 was the biggest motor, and that was a pretty sorry performance situation for two to three years there. But [the Berlinetta] was a car that, if you look into the advertising aspect, was put together to appeal primarily to the women. We thought of it as the first postwar advertising campaign aimed at the female market.

With the overall size and weight of the new platform reduced, for the first time ever Chevrolet bolted a four-

Showing off its elegant lines, an '88 convertible poses with its IROC sibling. The droptops returned in 1987 after a long hiatus. Only 1,007 of the more than 130,000 Camaro buyers jumped at the offer of an open-air cruiser. The following year, Chevrolet offered RPO 1LE, a special performance package that created an SCCA Showroom Stock class racer in street guise.

OPPOSITE: Along with the 1991 name change came new styling for the body cladding. A taller rear-deck spoiler and a pair of raised scoops on the hood replaced the previous louvered scoops.

When Chevrolet didn't sign up their 1991 as the car of choice for the IROC race series, it lost the rights to use the series name as a model and the Z28 arrived as its replacement.

cylinder to the engine mounts under the hood. Taken from the Pontiac Division, the Iron Duke displaced 151 cubic inches and produced a paltry 90 horsepower. It was the standard engine in the sports coupe! Thankfully, this anemic base engine was supplanted by a V6 four years later, in 1986.

As the end of the '80s drew near, the big news was that in 1987 the 350 would return, renewing the hope in the minds of speed freaks that performance was returning to Detroit's machines. Along with the return of the 350, which pushed the performance threshold back up to 225 net horsepower, came the offering of a convertible model, something that had been seen last in 1969. Because of inherent structural problems in the convertibles, which manifested in the physical form of cowl flex (an undesirable characteristic in which the body structure flexes at the cowl/rocker panel juncture, resulting in steering-column

movement, windshield bowing, and jarring ride qualities over rough roads), the 350 was not available in convertible models from the factory.

The Z28 and the Berlinetta models bowed out in 1987, replaced by the IROC-Z model and an LT option for the base sports coupe that lasted but a single year. The new IROC-Z, which lured those in their late teens and early twenties in a manner that hadn't been seen in decades, was based on a race series, the International Race of Champions. IROC had been around since 1973, a series designed to pit the best drivers from various motorsports categories against each other in identically prepared cars.

From 1975 until 1990, the series utilized the Camaro, providing market visibility and the unique situation in which drivers of cars from competing manufacturers were seated behind the wheels of Bowtie products. Who won the first IROC race, held at Riverside International Raceway? It was-

PAGES 84–85: Do you think Chevrolet kept the youth market in mind even though it had been targeting the female and upscale markets extensively? The 1983 Camaro IROC-ZR show car is a definite "yes" answer to that question.

none other than Mark Donohue (though driving a Porsche), of course, eventually winning three of the four races that season and taking the very first IROC title. (The first IROC season began in late '73 and ended in '74, and thus was considered a '74 series.) When the contract for the IROC series went to the Dodge Avenger in 1991, the 1990 IROC-Z was replaced by the 1991 Z28. Along the way, the IROC-Z's 350 had gradually been bumped up to 230 horsepower, then in 1990 to 245. By 1985, both the Cross-Fire and throttle-body injection systems had been replaced by Tuned Port injection, a more reliable fuel system that offered better throttle response. This would be the top-rated mill of the '80s and early '90s, but when the new Camaro debuted in 1993, it would bring even more hope for the power hungry.

Chevrolet also proved that it still had a few of those "back door" racing tricks up its sleeves. In 1989 an option package was created for the SCCA's latest race category, Showroom Stock. Coded 1LE, the package consisted of disc brakes at all corners, an exhaust system with dual catalytic converters that eliminated the shared converter and is considered a "true dual" system, an engine oil cooler, and performance tires.

This package was available to drivers who specified on the order form an IROC-Z combined with the RPO G92 performance rear-axle option. For those IROC-Zs ordered with air-conditioning, the 1LE package was built into the car as a street machine. Without air-conditioning, the IROCs were built for the racetrack with a lighter aluminum driveshaft, revised damping, higher-capacity fuel pump with an anti-slosh baffle in the fuel tank to prevent fuel starvation during hard cornering under race conditions, and heavy-duty front brakes. The deletion of the foglights from the front fascia also increased the airflow to the radiator for better cooling, an important consideration in a race car. Even though it started out as a little-known option designed for a few racers, to this day, 1LE Camaros can be ordered by the general public, as long as the buyer knows the proper option combinations.

Through most of the ten-year production span of the third-generation Camaro, structural chassis revisions were minor and limited to enhancing the car's road mannerisms. Sheetmetal revisions were confined to the nose and tail, with new fasciae featuring subtle changes and the rear spoiler changing from a low, hatch-mounted piece reminiscent of the spoilers of the first generation to a tall, two-pillared piece on the 1991 Z28 Camaros. Chevrolet also began combining options under group packages, simplifying the ordering process.

Camaro sales during the 1980s were a frightening roller-coaster ride. From a high in 1984, when more than a quarter-million of the new F-bodies sold, the model year 1990 set a new low for the Camaro, with just under 35,000 units moving off dealers' lots. This was a worse sales total than those during the years of the oil embargo and UAW strikes.

After some limited market testing in 1987–88, the Rally Sport returned to the lineup in 1989 as the base model and stayed in that position until the final year (1992) of third-generation Camaro production. In 1990 the interior, which reflected the angular exterior lines with flat interior surfaces, got a new airbag-equipped steering wheel, thanks to the federally mandated passive restraint systems. That final year was also the twenty-fifth anniversary of the sports coupe, and it was commemorated with a special Heritage Package option. This anniversary option featured twin over-the-hood-and-trunk stripes, body-color grille, black-out treatment, and special badging; more than ten percent of 1992 Camaros sold were built with this package. In the power train department, the engine options remained unchanged, but not for long.

Although they were important in the evolution of the Camaro, the third-generation Camaros are not given their due for a number of reasons. The majority are still on the road, used as daily drivers. Many are used in various forms of racing and can be found at drag strips with wildly modified engines. In one way, the situation is reminiscent of the late '70s and early '80s, when enthusiasts were more concerned with patching the rust and tweaking the mill for speed. Restoration to correct period status isn't a concern, as it is now with the first- and second-generation Camaros. But I suspect that the day when it will be is not far off.

Many feel that the 1992 models are the best of the third-generation Camaros. This '92 RS Heritage model (RPO Z03) shows off the body-color grille, blacked out headlamp buckets, twin hood and rear decklid stripes, and Heritage badging on the nose.

Something New, Something Old

The Latest F-car Redesign Shows a Return to Its Roots

6

Whereas the 1982–92 F-cars had turned to angularity for a new look, the latest iteration returned to its roots with more rounded surfaces than had been seen in a long time. In 1993, performance wasn't taking a place on the back burner any longer.

Both the interior and exterior of the car were extensively reworked, with the new shape taking on an even more sleek, continuous profile. The front end, which since the second generation had carried the sloped shovel-nose theme, now followed the curved hoodline, tapering to a point. The headlights were buried in recesses covered with flush-mounted covers. Turn signals and parking lights remained in the lower half of the fascia, which still carried the trademark Camaro center point. The tops of the fenders and rear quarter panels were no longer flat; instead, a graceful curve rolled down the side and eliminated the protruding angle at the belt line. The fenders also featured protrusions that picked up the bulk of the side mirrors, blending them into an aerodynamic profile with the fenders. Though the steeply raked windshield remained, the vast expanse of glass at the rear hatch was made shorter and steeper. While the car was still a hatchback, the new rear end, which extended a few feet past the glass, gave the appearance of a trunk.

Overall, the new look of the Camaro carried the aerodynamic styling of the previous version a step further. Following this new styling theme was a new interior. Gone were the flat surfaces of the earlier generation, replaced by rounded, soft profiles. Analog gauges remained, though. It seemed the digital-gauge fiasco of the third generation's Berlinettas was a lesson that had been remembered.

The rear suspension used a design similar to the earlier version's, but up front, a short-and-long-arm-style (SLA) front suspension added to the near-mythical handling characteristics of the F-car.

Power for the Z28 version came from a new 350, coded the LT1. Based on the Corvette LT1, the Camaro's version put out less power (275 hp) than the Vette's, but it was still an improvement over the previous year's output rating. The base models still carried a V6 under the hood, though displacement was upped to 207 cubic inches and output increased to 160 horsepower. No convertibles were offered in the first year of production for the latest platform. However, T-tops remained as popular as ever, with some ten percent of the 39,000 Camaros produced in 1993 so equipped.

The big additions the following year were the introduction of a power-operated convertible top model and a new six-speed gearbox built by Borg-Warner. Though a solid

OPPOSITE: Presenting a view that any Mustang owner would dread to have loom large in his rearview mirror, this 1997 thirtieth-anniversary SS displays the functional hood scoop that upped the performance of the 350-cube LT1 engine to 305 horsepower and was part of the SS conversion carried out by Street Legal Performance.

Callaway Cars, a Conneticut-based supertuner best known for creating otherworldly performing Corvettes, also handled a few Camaros. This example happens to be a 1994 version that, once tweaked, offered far greater oomph than its production cousins.

performer, the new six-speed did include one thing that most owners came to hate: a computer-aided gear selection (CAGS) function. Essentially a device to help keep the car compliant with target fuel economy goals, CAGS forced the driver to go from first to fourth gear during low-rpm shifts. Fortunately, the aftermarket responded with a resistor-equipped plug-in wiring harness that fooled the computer when it was in the CAGS mode, allowing first-to-second shifts at any rpm.

The 1995 Camaro saw continuing sales increases, making it back to the 120,000-plus mark. Other than the addition of a traction control system (Acceleration Slip Regulation) that used both braking and engine power modulation when wheel slip was detected, changes were minimal. Halfway through the year, an optional 3.8-liter V6 was offered that pumped out an impressive (for its size) 200 horsepower.

It was in 1996 that several important additions were made. The Rally Sport returned as a separate model, and, true to its past, it was a cosmetic treatment that differentiated itself from the base model with RS-only fascia, sills, and rear spoiler. The new 3.8-liter replaced the earlier V6 as the standard engine in both the base and RS models, but the really big news of '96 was that the Super Sport was back. Instead of being an engine-package change performed by Chevrolet on the assembly line, the new SSes were contracted out to Street Legal Performance (SLP) Engineering, a Montreal-based aftermarket tuner and converter.

These SSes were based on the Z28s and attainable by checking off the boxes for RPO R7T (SS), QLC (P245/50ZR-16 tires), and GU5 (Performance Axle Ratio, required with automatics only) when filling out the order form. The LT1 350 was left in stock form, but the Z28 hood was replaced with a NACA-ducted hood with functional ram air plumbing. The induction modifications, along with the porting of the

A 1994 Z28 strikes a proud and powerful pose. Coupled to the 350-cubic-inch small-block is a Borg-Warner six-speed gearbox, which helped the

As the fourth-generation Camaros were refined, their lines reflected the smooth styling trends of the '90s. This '95 Z28 shows off the package's five

In 1994, the first of the fourth-generation convertibles debuted; this one happens to be painted in Polo Green Metallic. Note the subtly styled integral rear spoiler.

stock exhaust manifolds, bumped the horsepower rating to the three hundred level (305) for the first time in decades. An optional exhaust system added another five to that total, if you wished. The sport suspension of the package combined with its Corvette-style 17x9-inch (43x23cm) alloy rims and short-sidewall P245/40-ZR17 tires offered a stiff ride that, though uncomfortable on rough roads, stuck like glue in the corners.

It may seem to be a contradiction, but customers didn't actually get the 16-inch (40.5cm) tires that option QLC indicated. That option instead triggered the inclusion of the 150-mph (240km) speedometer and the unlimited-top-speed engine computer. Gearshift duties in the SS were assigned to a Hurst shifter and linkage. Other than the ducted hood, the only exterior distinction of the SS models were the fender-mounted SS badges. It had taken too long, but finally a production street car that could tick off low-13-second ETs in the quarter-mile had been returned to the hands of hot rodders. Surprisingly, though, overall production totals fell through the floor overnight, with just over 60,000 Camaros making it to the showroom floors.

The 1997 model lineup continued unchanged with the exception of an interior redesign of the instrument panel and refined seats for better support. The addition of a thirtieth-anniversary edition was the highlight of the '97 models. As outlined in chapter 8, this anniversary edition

was chosen to pace the Brickyard 400. Both the pair of pace cars built specifically for the race and the regular production thirtieth-anniversary editions sported twin Hugger Orange racing stripes, reminiscent of those offered on the '69 pace cars. Interior appointments were done in white leather, with commemorative logos stitched into the headrests.

It wasn't until 1998 that the circle of performance was completed. Taking the Corvette-derived all-aluminum 350 (coded LS1) and offering it in the Z28 was the icing on the cake. Without having to go the SS route, buyers were again put into the low-13-second quarter-mile zone. Even though it features an overhead-valve-pushrod design that's considered by most in the industry to be primitive in terms of engine development, the LS1 satisfied even the most torque-hungry with its 335 lbs.-ft. of torque (4,000 rpm) and 305 hp (5,200 rpm).

Included with the all-aluminum mill (which also featured

The LT1 350 shown here in a 1994 Z28 featured a new fuel-delivery system referred to as Sequential Fuel Injection. It pumped out 275-horsepower at the rear wheels. It would be the top mill until the LS1 350 was bolted between the strut towers in 1998.

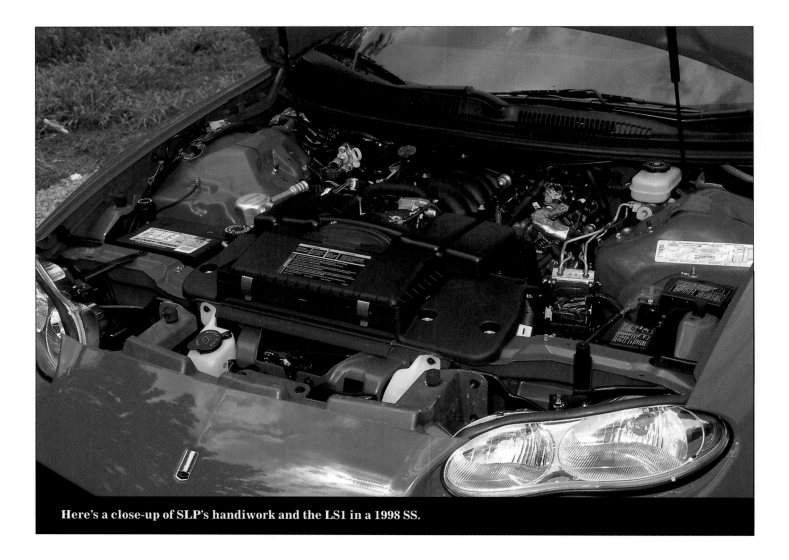

Here's a close-up of SLP's handiwork and the LS1 in a 1998 SS.

four-bolt main caps and a nodular-iron crankshaft) came a revolutionary composite plastic intake manifold. Not only did this piece help performance with its lighter weight, but the inherent qualities of the composite material help keep the incoming air charge much cooler than did its metal fore-bears. After hot-lapping an LS1, one can actually pop the hood and lay a hand on the manifold without getting burned. That, my friends, is efficient, to say the least!

With so much power now getting to the ground, braking was revised, with larger disc brakes and refinement to the Acceleration Slip Regulation system. An aluminum drive-shaft and Torsen heavy-duty limited-slip differential also complemented the Z28's LS1 package. As good as all that may sound, the SS models made it better yet. No longer

handled by SLP, the 1998 SSes were done in-house by Chevrolet. The option package remained the same, with the LS1 subtly tweaked to boost horsepower up to the 320 mark. Additional SS options, however (Hurst shifter, Bilstein suspension, free-flow exhaust), still had to be installed by SLP at its Canadian facility.

For looks, all Camaro models in 1998 as well as 1999 feature a new nose that eliminates the flush-mounted head-light covers in favor of recessed joint "quad" headlamps with a "double-bubble" contour line following the headlight curvature along the length of the hood. The front fascia is no longer split into upper and lower halves; instead, just below the center peak is a cavernous faux grille with a black plastic insert and openings off to the sides. To the grille's

Extensively revised for the 1998 model year, the Camaro's nose featured a cavernous grille opening filled with a black plastic insert and a sculpted hood that picked up the twin headlamp lines.

As the twenty-first century draws near, Camaro performance is coming on strong. Like the cowl-inducted-hood-equipped Z28s of the first generation, this 1998 SS offers a hint of its capabilities with the package's functional ducted hood.

OPPOSITE: A base 1998 Sport Coupe displays more than three decades of evolutionary and revolutionary ponycar design in its lines. Many enthusiasts don't realize how close the barn doors came to permanently closing on this legendary performer.

sides are the turn signals, and below are foglamp openings.

For 1999, Chevrolet has brought the same line to the market, adding a limited-production SS convertible to the lineup. With advertisements that hype the SS as "SS.

Camaro, taken to its logical extreme," it's easy to see that Chevrolet hasn't forgotten what makes the Camaro the true love of die-hard ponycar enthusiasts. Let's just hope that it keeps the good times rolling.

The Trans-Am Saga

The Camaro Takes Command of the SCCA's Ponycar Corral

"**W**in on Sunday, sell on Monday." This is perhaps one of the oldest, best-known adages of the automotive industry. It was a concept Chevrolet, or any car manufacturer for that matter, could not ignore. Ford had beaten the Bowtie gang to the punch, launching the first-ever ponycar, and had enjoyed two full production years with virtually no marketplace competition.

Shortly after the debut of the Mustang, the Sports Car Club of America (SCCA) in 1966 developed a new category of road course racing aimed primarily at production road-going sedans of the day, the Trans-American Sedan Championship (Trans-Am). Sports car racing was nothing new to the SCCA. Races had been run for years at former military bases and airfields, as well as the usual race circuits. But these races were dominated by low-slung two-seaters and, with the exception of the Chevrolet Corvette and Shelby Cobra, most of the race fields were filled with European roadsters, to which the average American didn't really relate. What was lacking was a class in which a car more identifiable to the masses could compete.

Of course NASCAR, an entity with absolutely no ties to the SCCA, had the "stock car" approach pretty well sewn up by this time. But while NASCAR's stockers were selected from intermediate-sized car platforms and stuffed with the biggest engine allowable, Trans-Am took a different angle.

Entries would be limited to those sedans officially recognized and homologated by the international motorsports governing body, the FIA–Federal International Automobile–as being regular production sedans. One interesting note is that the production requirement for homologation during the first few years of Trans-Am was a thousand cars. How did Chevrolet get the Z/28 legalized with a production run of only 602? Apparently, the competition did not lodge a protest, and the matter was either never investigated or the Z/28 was allowed to run in order to provide a more competitive field that season! The rules were later changed to allow any production sedan, regardless of totals. Initially, there were two categories, the first for cars with engines displacing more than two liters, the second for those under the two-liter mark. In 1969 Trans-Am would run only one class, keeping the competition limited to American-built ponycars.

Trans-Am's limiting of engine displacement may have kept overall top speeds down, but top speed wasn't the only way to win a race. With the majority of the circuits comprised of short straightaways connected with tight left-hand and right-hand turns, handling, braking, and balance were at a premium. This fact would play into the hands of the Camaro teams from the beginning.

As far as modifications were concerned, the rules stated that other than items required in the interest of safety, pretty much all else had to be stock or available to the general public. (This rule can be credited with creating some of the

OPPOSITE: Fielded by Mark Donohue and Craig Fisher, the '67 shown here lacks the Penske/Sunoco lettering that later became synonymous with winning Trans-Am entries. This action is from the 1967 Sebring endurance race. By the way, they won.

most valuable, incredible street cars that have ever been driven on a public roadway.) Of course, performance tuning and the substitution of certain items (such as shocks, springs, and rims) were allowed as long as such replacement components were mounted in the factory locations or kept the factory dimensions (e.g., the use of magnesium rims to save weight).

This new form of racing, which seemed designed expressly for the new ponycars then emerging from Detroit, debuted with its first full season in 1966. Ironically, though, the first-ever Trans-Am victory wouldn't go to an American car manufacturer. Instead, Jochen Rindt, who would later earn a reputation in Formula 1 (F1), won the first Trans-Am race, held at Sebring Raceway in Sebring, Florida. Ford's Mustang eventually took the Manufacturer's Championship that year as well as the following year, 1967.

The Camaros that carried the Chevrolet banner didn't look like the type of factory-backed racer today's race fans are used to. Though some big-name sponsors did step in to assist, by and large the factory had to refrain from directly supporting the race effort — or at least appear to. The most famous of the Camaro teams was the Penske/Sunoco operation. With driver Mark Donohue behind the wheel and Roger Penske's organizational and performance abilities dictating the team's development, Ford wouldn't be holding the title for long. And the team had an ace hidden up its sleeve: Vince Piggins, head of Chevrolet's product performance group. This was an engineering team that pretty much had lost its teeth with the AMA ban on corporate involvement in racing, but when the SCCA's Trans-Am class heated up the ponycar wars, Piggins was quietly given a small staff to work with. With Donohue's seat-of-the-pants feedback, Piggins and his team of engineers developed several important components of the famed Z28 package that made it possible for Chevrolet to win the championship in its second season of competition.

This brings us back to the first line of this chapter. Every time Piggins and his group developed something for the Penske/Sunoco operation, it had to be made available to the customer as an option. You want tubular exhaust head-

ers for reduced backpressure and better performance? Four-wheel power disc brakes to get deep in a corner to pass a competitor? Dual-quad cross-ram intake manifold for better mid- to high-rpm response? You know what? The average Joe had better be able to get his hands on this stuff or the technical inspectors wouldn't pass your car. Well, the average Joe could get his speed-hungry hands on these parts — and did.

Donohue Domination

The Mustang had taken the 1967 Trans-Am Manufacturer's Championship title for Ford, primarily by virtue of being further along in its high-performance development routine when Trans-Am was born. So Chevrolet had to play catch-up again, and did so well. Despite the late entry into the series, Donohue in the Team Penske/Sunoco–backed Camaro drove to three victories late in the 1967 season. In 1968 there were no fewer than ten victories, all with the legendary Donohue in the driver's seat.

The first of these victories came at Sebring, the last at Pacific Raceways. For the remainder of the season, no other name but Donohue's would appear in the winner's circle along with the Chevrolet logo. Donohue came to Penske with an extensive racing background. Three class championship titles were already notched on his belt by the time he came to Trans-Am. And he didn't limit his competitiveness to the Trans-Am series, either. He clinched the U.S. Road Racing Championship series in both '67 and '68. During the 1969 season, he also qualified for the Indianapolis 500, finishing in seventh place and earning the United States Auto Championship Rookie of the Year designation. The next year, he'd take runner-up honors at the Brickyard, and in 1972 he conquered that great race and drank the ceremonial milk in the Indianapolis winner's circle.

After leaving Team Penske/Sunoco for American Motors Corporation (AMC) in 1970, Donohue went on to help capture the title for AMC. This season was perhaps the most

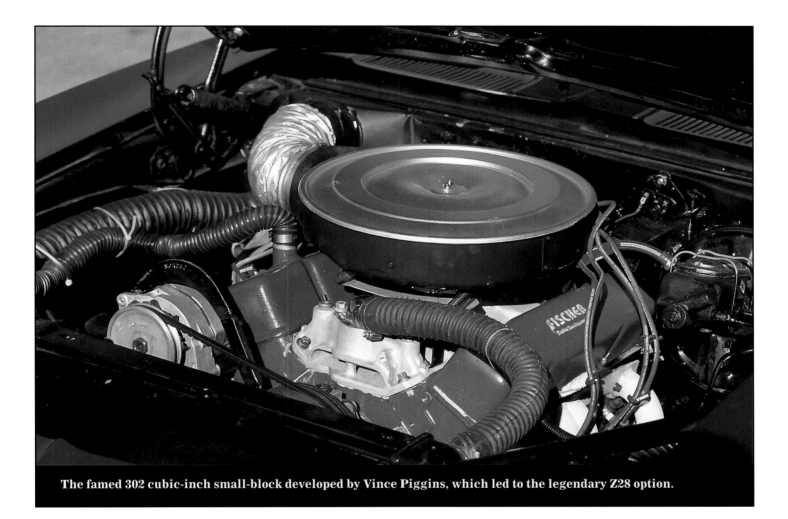

The famed 302 cubic-inch small-block developed by Vince Piggins, which led to the legendary Z28 option.

memorable, with full factory support finally reaching the series. By the end of his Trans-Am career, he had won twenty-nine races of the fifty-five he'd entered, a record that has yet to be equaled. Drivers in the awe-inspiring Canadian American Challenge cars also found themselves dicing against Donohue, who it seemed could find success no matter what type of car he was racing. He'd started in that series in 1966 with a second-place championship finish and left it with the 1973 championship honors. Along the way, he did for Porsche what he'd done for Chevrolet and the Camaro — made it a one-man, one-make show. Behind the wheel of Porsche's 917/30 Panzer, he swept the 1973 season, winning six of the eight races held. It was seemingly a good time to retire, especially given that he was raising a son.

The only place victory had eluded him was in Formula 1,

the holy grail of auto racing. Attempting two races in North America in 1971, Donohue could muster no better than a third-place finish in the Canadian Grand Prix. In 1974 he came out of his short retirement and made two fruitless attempts at F1, but he held on to hopes for the coming season. In 1975 he crashed during practice for the Austrian Grand Prix. The incident claimed the life of a course marshal and injured another. Donohue, though seemingly unhurt, fell into a coma and died within days, bringing a tragic end to a short yet very full career, one that has given the names Donohue and Trans-Am special meaning.

The close of the decade would signal the end of absolute dominance in Trans-Am by the Camaro. It would take another fourteen years for the Camaro to rise once again to the top of Trans-Am and dominate the way it had in the

PAGES 104–105: A quiet moment in the pits for Donohue's famed number 6 Camaro.

early years. When Donohue was driving, he graced the top spot on the podium no fewer than six times in 1969, and for the first time, another Camaro driver appeared in the winner's circle: Ron Bucknam, who raced to victory twice. Of course, this second full season of Trans-Am for the Camaro was the second year in a row that Chevrolet would claim the Manufacturer's Championship.

Disaster for this phenomenal racing introduction came only a few short years after its first title, when its star driver moved to another team and manufacturer. The first season of the new decade saw Camaros fielded against stronger teams. The new 350-cubic-inch engine-displacement rule resulted in the demise of the beloved 302 that had spawned the Z/28, and Chevy's ubiquitous small-block 350 was used in its place. Ford ruled the roost that year, and the following year Donohue had taken his place in the driver's seat of an AMC Javelin. Again, Donohue was at his finest, taking the title from Ford and giving it to the tiny upstart manufacturer.

The 1970 Trans-Am season was a precursor for the even worse times that lay ahead. Two victories — that's it. The following year, none. The year after — again, none. Then, a brief glimmer of hope in 1973: two victories early in the season. Unfortunately those were followed by another drought. Once again, Camaros went winless for two straight years. Between '73 and '83, there would be only ten victories for the Camaro. But 1983 turned out to be the banner year for the Camaro, with ten victories shared among three drivers and Chevrolet taking the Manufacturer's Championship. Coincidentally, it was, like 1968, the second year of production of an entirely new design.

Along the way, Trans-Am had undergone changes in car classification, endured the gas crunch with a three-race season in 1974, and seen a host of victories go to Porsche. In 1980 the SCCA had changed its method of classifying cars, choosing a simple engine-displacement-to-weight format. Though the bodies of the cars resembled what average Americans saw at their dealerships, that's where the similarities ended. Under the production skin, all-out tube-chassied racers lurked, ones that couldn't be gotten from the factory for the street, that's for sure!

After 1983, wins would again be hard to come by, and it wasn't until Scott Sharp got behind the wheel in 1991 that the Camaro would reclaim its crown. Sharp's first victory in Mexico gave the Camaro its fiftieth Trans-Am win, and Chevrolet its one hundredth. When and where the Camaro hadn't been winning, the Corvette quite often had. Even if both Scott Sharp and Jack Baldwin drove Camaros, it was certain that there weren't any "team orders" being followed between these two. The 1992 Driver's Championship went to Baldwin in the last turn of the last race. Baldwin's second-place finish to Sharp's third put him just four points over Sharp, but that was enough to claim the title. Sharp, however, returned the following season in top form, winning six races to Baldwin's two and reclaiming the title. The second half of the 1990s saw new names racing Camaros, and Ron Fellows brought home enough points in 1995 for Chevrolet to again claim the Manufacturer's Championship, the last one to date for the Camaro.

As of this writing, the Chevrolet Camaro tops the list as the winningest Trans-Am model ever raced, with eighty-seven victories. In 1997, Ford pulled ahead of Chevrolet with thirteen consecutive victories, but Chevrolet still holds the record for the most pole positions earned — 120 — and the fastest race laps set, at fifty-five. Not too bad considering that the illustrious ponycar spent the early part of its career playing catch-up!

Camaro SCCA Trans-Am Titles

Year	Title
1968	Manufacturer's Championship
1969	Manufacturer's Championship
1983	Manufacturer's Championship
1991	Manufacturer's Championship
1991	Driver's Championship, Scott Sharp
1992	Manufacturer's Championship
1992	Driver's Championship, Jack Baldwin
1993	Manufacturer's Championship
1993	Driver's Championship, Scott Sharp
1995	Manufacturer's Championship

SCCA Trans-Am Victories

Date	Track	Driver	Date	Track	Driver
8/13/67	Marlboro Speedway	Mark Donohue	6/21/86	Detroit	Wally Dallenbach, Jr.
10/1/67	Stardust Raceway	Mark Donohue	7/13/86	Mid-Ohio	Greg Pickett
10/8/67	Pacific Raceways	Mark Donohue	9/28/86	Sears Point Raceway	Wally Dallenbach, Jr.
3/22/68	Sebring	Mark Donohue	5/29/88	Sears Point Raceway	Willy T. Ribbs
		Craig Fisher	5/19/91	Mexico City	Scott Sharp
5/12/68	War Bonnet Park	Mark Donohue	6/15/91	Detroit	Scott Sharp
5/30/68	Lime Rock Park	Mark Donohue	7/12/91	Des Moines	George Robinson
6/16/68	Mid-Ohio	Mark Donohue	8/10/91	Watkins Glen	Scott Sharp
6/23/68	Bridgehampton	Mark Donohue	8/18/91	Trois Rivieres	Scott Sharp
7/7/68	Meadowdale Raceway	Mark Donohue	9/8/91	Mosport Park	Scott Sharp
7/21/68	Mt. Tremblant	Mark Donohue	9/21/91	Road America	Scott Sharp
8/4/68	Bryar Motorsport Park	Mark Donohue	10/20/91	Texas World Speedway	Jack Baldwin
8/25/68	Continental Divide Raceway	Mark Donohue	6/20/92	Portland	Paul Gentilozzi
10/6/68	Pacific Raceways	Mark Donohue	6/28/92	Mosport Park	Scott Sharp
6/8/69	Mid-Ohio	Ron Bucknam	7/12/92	Des Moines	Scott Sharp
7/20/69	Bryar Motorsport Park	Mark Donohue	8/8/92	Watkins Glen	Jack Baldwin
8/3/69	Mt. Tremblant	Mark Donohue	8/16/92	Trois Rivieres	Jack Baldwin
8/10/69	Watkins Glen	Mark Donohue	9/12/92	Mid-Ohio	Greg Pickett
8/24/69	Laguna Seca	Mark Donohue	10/4/92	Sears Point Raceway	Darrin Brassfield
9/7/69	Seattle Raceway	Ron Bucknam	6/20/93	Mosport Park	Scott Sharp
9/21/69	Sears Point Raceway	Mark Donohue	7/4/93	Sears Point Raceway	Scott Sharp
10/5/69	Riverside Raceway	Mark Donohue	7/17/93	Toronto	Scott Sharp
7/5/70	Donnybrooke Speedway	Milt Minter	8/7/93	Watkins Glen	Scott Sharp
8/16/70	Watkins Glen	Vic Elford	8/15/93	Trois Rivieres	Scott Sharp
6/16/73	Watkins Glen	Maurice Carter	8/21/93	Road America	Scott Sharp
7/15/73	Sanair Raceway	Warren Agor	9/4/93	Mid-Ohio	Jack Baldwin
7/24/76	Road America	Carl Shafer	9/19/93	Dallas	Jack Baldwin
8/15/76	Brainerd International Raceway	Carl Shafer	5/22/94	Mosport Park	Scott Pruett
5/6/79	Rodriguez Autodrome	Miguel Muniz	7/9/94	Cleveland	Scott Pruett
8/23/80	Trois Rivieres	Roy Woods	8/28/94	Atlanta	Scott Pruett
10/11/81	Laguna Seca	George Follmer	5/6/95	Phoenix	Price Cobb
5/15/83	Summit Point Raceway	David Hobbs	6/10/95	Detroit	Ron Fellows
6/5/83	Sears Point Raceway	David Hobbs	6/18/95	Portland	Ron Fellows
6/12/83	Portland International Raceway	Willy T. Ribbs	7/22/95	Cleveland	Ron Fellows
7/17/83	Mid-Ohio	Willy T. Ribbs	8/6/95	Trois Rivieres	Ron Fellows
7/31/83	Road America	David Hobbs	8/12/95	Watkins Glen	Ron Fellows
8/8/83	Brainerd International Raceway	Willy T. Ribbs	2/25/96	St. Petersburg	Ron Fellows
9/4/83	Trois Rivieres	John Paul, Jr.	4/14/96	Long Beach	Jamie Galles
9/18/83	Sears Point Raceway	Willy T. Ribbs	5/19/96	Mosport Park	Paul Gentilozzi
9/25/83	Riverside Raceway	David Hobbs	8/4/96	Trois Rivieres	Ron Fellows
10/8/83	Caesar's Palace	Willy T. Ribbs	9/1/96	Dallas	Ron Fellows
6/1/86	Sears Point Raceway	Wally Dallenbach, Jr.	9/22/96	Reno	Ron Fellows
6/14/86	Portland International Raceway	Wally Dallenbach, Jr.	8/15/98	Road America	Stu Hayner

Pacing Perfection

Three Generations Lead the Charge Around the Brickyard's Famed Banking

Being chosen to pace the Indianapolis 500 race, held every Memorial Day weekend, is one of the top honors that can be bestowed upon an automobile and its manufacturer. On race day, tens of thousands at the race get an eyeful of the selected model; in addition, millions of television viewers will likely get an even closer view as the pace car makes its parade laps, starts the field, and is called to duty during caution periods. Basically, it's every car company's ultimate advertising dream come true.

When it comes to the pace cars, once a particular make and model has been chosen, several examples are taken and modified for use at the track. Both safety and performance modifications are in order because not only will the chosen car be taking an obligatory parade lap (usually with a former racer at the wheel and a model and other dignitaries along for the ride), but these cars will be called to the front of the field whenever a caution arises. They'll need to handle corners better than the average road-going version and also be able to bring the race cars up to speed, then get out of the way as the track goes green.

Thus, the actual pace cars and the subsequent replicas offered for sale to the general public are different. Most of the safety and performance modifications made to the half-dozen or so pace cars used in the race don't carry over to the production version. What the buyer gets instead is typically a unique, sometimes gaudy paint scheme with graphics package and commemorative badging. Usually a certification plaque is affixed to the dash or console, and the exterior treatment will carry over to the interior in the form of matching color seats, which sometimes have embroidered pace car logos.

Though it doesn't sound like much, the allure of the pace car package is that it's always a limited production offering and can be combined with other pace cars and limited or special editions to make a unique collection. For Chevrolet, the first time the Camaro was so honored was in 1967—like the Mustang, in its first year of production. The '67 pacers were based on RS/SS convertibles, with the identification done in blue to match the SS nose stripe ("Chevrolet Camaro" in gold script above the blue Official Pace Car lettering on the doors). Inside, there weren't any special plaques or badges but instead a matching blue interior with blue upholstery offset by a pair of white stripes, which gave this particular pace car treatment a very tasteful look.

Power for the few cars (some sources say three, others say four) that were built for actual track duty was supplied by the 396 big-block linked to a floor-shifted Turbo Hydro-matic. The other one hundred or so replicas that were built weren't actually for sale to the public as an option this time around. Instead, they were reserved for use by race officials, Chevrolet, and VIPs. After the race, they passed into the public market as used cars. If you bought a used '67 pace car back then and still have it, you've made one of the deals

Like it's rival, the Mustang, the Camaro was chosen to pace the Indianapolis 500 in its introductory year.

of the century. Powertrain selections for the replicas aren't known in any exact form but were based on the SS option and were likely built with both 350- and 396-cubic-inch engines. Given the honor of piloting the pace car during the race was none other than Mauri Rose, a three-time winner of the race in the late 1940s.

When in 1969 the Camaro was again selected to lead the field to the start of what had become known as the "greatest spectacle in racing," Chevrolet did things a little bit differently. Again, RS/SS convertibles were used; this time, however, the graphics package was bolder, with orange lettering. Instead of the Bumblebee nose stripe, these cars sported twin racing stripes in matching orange and ZL2 cowl-induction hoods. The powertrain choices remained the same, but inside, the new-for-'69 houndstooth check seat fabric, in a bright orange-and-black pattern, blended nicely with the wood-grain finish on the dashboard. And this time around, Chevrolet capitalized on the honor by offering both coupe and convertible pace car option packages, and just under 4,000 of RPOs Z10 and Z11 (as they were catalogued) made it to buyers as new cars. Driving duty for the race was bestowed upon 1960 Indy winner Jim Rathmann.

No second-generation Camaros made it to the elevated status of pace car, but the first year of the third generation, 1982, brought the Camaro once again to the forefront at Indy. Because of the stranglehold that emissions and economy had placed on the Camaro by this time, the '82s had to undergo more extensive modifications to effectively perform their duties than had their predecessors. Based on the Z28 model, the silver/blue two-tone paint treatment was unique to the pacers. Again, Rathmann was the man behind the wheel during the race.

Carrying the winged tire logo of Indianapolis Raceway on the rear pillar, the '82's graphics were actually a bit less bold than the '69's. The scripted "Chevrolet Camaro" was dropped from the door, replaced with a lithographic-style Indianapolis 500 decal. Under the hood, the pair of real pace cars featured aluminum blocks, LT1 heads, and modified exhaust systems to make the power necessary to get up to the speeds required. For the 6,360 replicas that went to selected dealers, buyers could get either cross-ram fuel-injected or carbureted 305s under the hood. Inside the blue-and-silver cloth interior, a host of options ensured that where the performance was lacking, the creature comforts were not.

Eleven years later, the first of the latest Camaro redesigns was tapped for the job. Whereas the previous three pacers had performed their missions with an elegant, almost understated look, the 1993 pacers flat out screamed, "I'm going to Indy. Nyah, nyah!"

Four-color stripes split the white lower half and black upper half of the body just above the flank line. These weren't your average pinstripes, either. Starting as four stacked lines of color each about an inch tall, they went across the full nose width and down the body side, then flared out and began criss-crossing at the doors, making their way as separate wide stripes to the tail. A pair on the hood did the same, widening at the base of the windshield. For identification, the Indy logo was kept on the pillar, and a stylized IndyCar did a red-to-yellow fade on the door above the "Official Pace Car" lettering. The intertwining-stripe scheme was stitched into the seats, which were done in a plush, pace-only velourlike covering. As with the previous pacer, a host of option packages was required with the replica, which added $995 onto the window sticker. This year, instead of a former race winner at the wheel, the pace car circled the track at the hands of Chevrolet's general manager, Jim Perkins.

Perhaps the most noteworthy thing about the '93 version is that it brought with it the true spirit of the Z/28 of decades past. Other than the usual safety and communications modifications, the Z/28's 275-hp LT1 V8 was deemed powerful enough in stock form to pace the race. In a year often singled out as one where true performance returned to the Camaro, only 633 replicas were built, the lowest number since the '67 pace cars. If you just happen to own one of these, keep that in mind!

For the Camaro's thirtieth anniversary, in 1997, it was again honored with the designation as an official pace car, only this time it was for the third NASCAR race held at Indy, the Brickyard 400. As with the 1993 version, little had to be done performance-wise to bring the car up to the specifications required to make the fast trips around the Brickyard's oval. Other than changes made to the suspension to take into account Indy's nine-degree banking in the corners, these cars carried the same LT1s as the production versions, though they were balanced and blueprinted. A revised exhaust system also gave the actual pacers a bit more punch. Other than these few modifications, the replicas offered for sale under the thirtieth-anniversary package were not much different.

PAGES 112–113: The most recent Camaro designated as a pace car at the famed Brickyard was the 1993 model. Aside from safety and communications additions, not much was done to it, proving that performance had finally returned to a satisfactory level.

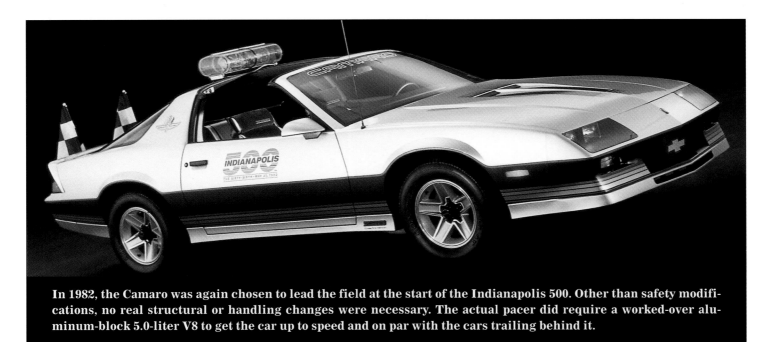

In 1982, the Camaro was again chosen to lead the field at the start of the Indianapolis 500. Other than safety modifications, no real structural or handling changes were necessary. The actual pacer did require a worked-over aluminum-block 5.0-liter V8 to get the car up to speed and on par with the cars trailing behind it.

OFFICIAL PACE CAR
77TH INDIANAPOLIS 500 · MAY 30, 1993.

Afterword

What Fate the F-body?

For several years now, Camaro enthusiasts and the press have wondered whether the Camaro will survive much past the millennium. Numerous reports, most based on rumor and speculation, have surfaced in various automotive magazines predicting the demise of the Camaro and its sister ship, the Firebird, in the year 2002. Why?

The Canadian United Auto Workers Union, representing the Ste. Therese, Quebec, plant, where the F-cars are currently built, has gone on record stating that the chassis will not be built at that facility after 2001. Of course, getting anyone in the know at GM or Chevrolet to discuss the car's future is pretty much impossible. The corporate statement, "We can't discuss future product," provides as much as we will know until the time comes when the boardroom decides to reveal more.

What is known is that the fourth-generation platform as we know it will not pass specific components of the safety regulations that are anticipated in the coming years. Recent speculation has also centered on the possibility that one of the F-cars will be dropped while the other soldiers on alone. Sales of the Firebird line during the past two to three years have been stronger than those of the Camaro, so if this rumor proves to be true, it doesn't look good for fans of the Bowtie; sales really are the bottom line in such a decision.

Yet as was pointed out to me recently, there likely is something better planned to either take its place or continue on as the fifth generation of the Camaro that we've all come to know and love. GM and Chevrolet will live on, with or without the Camaro, but for me, I hope to be behind the wheel of a stylistic standout come 2003 or 2004, one with a powerplant that produces gobs of torque and a sweet V8 howl for the ears, a gearbox that provides a satisfyingly solid shift accompanied by the smoky chirp of the tires — which, of course, should be independently suspended and nice and wide to hug the road. After all, I'll be in the car of my dreams, the Camaro, aka the Hugger, the thoroughbred of American ponycars.

OPPOSITE: This 1971 Sport Coupe is on the diminutive side, its white vinyl top providing a pleasing and understated contrast to its Nevada Silver paint. For some, raw power took a back seat to superior styling.

Further Reading

As stated in the introduction, this is not a numbers-crunching book aimed at those seeking to verify or restore their Camaros. During the writing of this book, the following titles were an invaluable resource for fact-checking and verification and are an excellent resource for anyone seeking additional information on the Chevrolet Camaro.

Schorr, Martyn L. *Camaro: Three Generations Of Premier Performance Cars*. Haworth, N.J.: Quicksilver Communications, 1982.

Guinn, Wayne D. *Camaro: Untold Secrets 1967–1969*. Driggs, Idaho: Tex Smith Publishing, 1991.

Antonick, Mike, ed. *The Genuine Camaro White Book 1967–1997*. Poewll, Ohio: Michael Bruce and Associates, 1996.

Car + Parts Magazine. *Catalog of Camaro ID Numbers 1967–93*. Sidney, Ohio: Amos Press, 1995.

Cunneen, Edward J. *COPO Camaros and Chevelles*. Lombard, Ill.: Np., nd.

Kowalke, Ron, and Beverly Rae Kimes, eds. *Standard Catalog of American Cars*. Np: Krause Publications, 1997.

MacNeish, Jerry. *The Definitive 1967–1968 Camaro Z/28 Fact Book*. Osceola, Wisc.: Motorbooks International, 1990.

Camaro Production Statistics

A By-the-Numbers Account of Thirty-two Years of Pride and Performance

First Generation

Style	Production	Price
1967		
Coupe	160,648	$2,572
Convertible	25,141	$2,809
Z28	602	$358.10
RS	64,842	$105.35
SS	34,411*	$210.65–$500.30
Pace Car	104**	N/A
Total	**220,906**	
1968		
Coupe	176,813	$2,670
Convertible	20,440	$2,908
Z28	7,199	$400.25
RS	40,977	$105.35
SS*	30,695	$210.65–$868.95
Total	**235,147**	
1969		
Coupe	165,226	$2,727
Convertible	17,573	$2,940
Z/28	20,302	$458.15
RS	37,773	$131.65
SS	36,309*	$295.95–$710.95
Pace Car	3,675	$36.90
Total	**243,085**	

Second Generation

Style	Production	Price
1970		
Coupe	100,967	$2,839
Z/28	8,733	$572.95
RS	27,136	$168.55
SS	15,201*	$289.65–$385.50
Total	**124,901**	
1971		
Coupe	91,481	$2,848
Z/28	4,862	$786.75
RS	18,404	$179.05
SS	18,287*	$313.90–$99.05
Total	**114,630**	

*Total includes both RPO Z27 SS package and optional SS engines sold. Price shown indicates RPO Z27 and highest-priced SS engine option.
**Total includes actual and replica Pace Cars produced.

1972
Coupe	58,544	$2,819
Z/28	2,575	$769.15
RS	11,364	$118
SS	7,532*	$306.35–96
Total	**68,651**	

1973
Coupe	52,850	$2,822.70
Z/28	11,574	$598.05
Type LT	32,327	$3,211.70
RS	16,133	$118
Total	**96,751**	

1974
Coupe	88,243	$3,039.70
Z/28	13,802	$572.05
Type LT	48,963	$3,380.70
Total	**151,008**	

1975
Coupe	105,927	$3,698.05
Type LT	39,843	$4,070
RS	7,000	$238
Total	**145,770**	

1976
Coupe	130,538	$3,927.35
Type LT	52,421	$4,320.35
RS	15,855	$260
Total	**182,959**	

1977
Coupe	131,717	$4,113.45
Z28	14,349	$5,170.06
Type LT	72,787	$4,478.45
RS	17,026	$281
Total	**218,853**	

1978
Coupe	134,491	$4,414.25
Z28	54,907	$5,603.85
Type LT	65,635	$4,814.25
Type LT/RS	5,696	$5,065.25
RS	11,902	$4,784.25
Total	**272,631**	

1979
Coupe	111,357	$4,676.90
Z28	84,877	$6,115.35
Berlinetta	67,236	$5,395.90
RS	19,101	$5,072.90
Total	**282,571**	

1980
Coupe	68,174	$5,498.60
Z28	45,137	$7,121.32
Berlinetta	26,679	$6,261.60
RS	12,015	$5,915.60
Total	**152,005**	

1981
Coupe	62,614	$6,581.23
Coupe Z28	20,253	$8,025.23
Berlinetta	43,272	$7,356.23
Total	**126,139**	

Third Generation

Style	Production	Price

1982
Style	Production	Price
Coupe	78,759	$8,029.50
Coupe Z28	64,882	$10,099.26
Berlinetta	39,744	$9,665.06
Pace Car	6,362*	$10,099.26
Total	**189,747**	

1983
Coupe	63,806	$8,036
Coupe Z28	62,650	$10,336
Berlinetta	27,925	$9,881
Total	**154,381**	

1984
Coupe	127,292	$7,995
Coupe Z28	100,899	$10,620
Berlinetta	33,400	$10,895
Total	**261,591**	

1985
Coupe	97,966	$8,363
Coupe Z28	68,403	$11,060
Berlinetta	13,649	$11,060
IROC	21,177	$659
Total	**180,018**	

1986
Coupe	99,608	$9,349
Coupe Z28	88,132	$12,316
Berlinetta	4,479	$12,316
IROC	49,585	$659
Total	**192,219**	

1987
Coupe	45,501	$10,409
Convertible	263	$15,208
Coupe Z28	52,863	$13,233
Convertible Z28	744	$17,632
IROC	38,889	$699–3,273
Total	**137,760**	

1988

Coupe	66,605	$10,995
Convertible	1,859	$16,255
Coupe IROC-Z	24,050	$13,490
Convertible IROC-Z	3,761	$18,015
Total	**96,275**	

1989

RS Coupe	83,487	$11,495
RS Convertible	3,245	$16,995
Coupe IROC-Z	20,067	$14,145
Convertible IROC-Z	3,940	$18,945
1LE	111	N/A
Total	**110,739**	

1990

RS Coupe	28,750	$10,995
RS Convertible	729	$16,880
Coupe IROC-Z	4,213	$14,555
Convertible IROC-Z	1,294	$10,195
Coupe 1LE	62	$675
Total	**34,986**	

1991

RS Coupe	79,854	$12,180
RS Convertible	5,329	$17,960
Coupe Z28	12,452	$15,445
Convertible Z28	3,203	$20,185
Coupe 1LE	478	$675
Total	**100,838**	

1992

RS Coupe	60,994	$12,075
RS Convertible	2,562	$18,055
Coupe Z28	5,197	$16,055
Convertible Z28	1,254	$21,500
Coupe 1LE	705	$675
Total	**70,007**	

Fourth Generation

1993

Style	Production	Price
Coupe	21,253	$21,253
Coupe Z28	17,850	$17,850
Pace Car	633*	$995
1LE	19	$310
Total	**39,103**	

1994

Coupe	76,531	$13,499
Coupe Z28	36,008	$16,999
Convertible	2,328	$18,745
Convertible Z28	4,932	$22,075
Coupe 1LE	135	$310
Total	**119,799**	

1995

Coupe	77,431	$14,250
Coupe Z28	30,335	$17,915
Convertible	6,948	$19,495
Convertible Z28	8,024	$23,095
Coupe 1LE	106	$310
Total	**122,738**	

1996

Coupe	31,528	$14,990
Coupe Z28	14,906	$19,390
Convertible	2,994	$21,270
Convertible Z28	2,938	$24,490
RS Coupe	8,091	$17,490
RS Convertible	905	$22,720
Coupe 1LE	55	$1,175
SS	2,410	$3,999
Total	**61,362**	

1997

Coupe	51,553	$16,215
Coupe Z28	17,955	$20,115
Convertible	8,647	$21,770
Convertible Z28	3,297	$25,520
RS Coupe	8,398	$17,970
RS Convertible	1,060	$23,170
Coupe 1LE	48	$1,175
Coupe SS	2,017	$3,999
Convertible SS	264	$3,999
30th Anniv. Coupe	3,476	$575
30th Anniv. Conv.	1,057	$575
Total	**60,200**	

1998

Coupe	49,343	$16,625
Coupe Z28	17,572	$20,470
Convertible	4,677	$22,125
Convertible Z28	2,480	$27,450
Camaro Coupe SS	3,025	N/A
Coupe 1LE	101	$1,348 (w Z28)
		$750 (w/o Z28)
Total	**54,020**	

Photo Credits

Automobile Quarterly Publications: pp. 12 left, 24, 50–51, 62, 65, 68–69, 70, 76–77, 80

©Bill Erdman: pp. 12–13, 48, 49, 57 inset, 60 top, 100, 108, 112–113

©Jerry Heasley: pp. 15, 21 top, 31, 32, 34, 35, 39 bottom., 44, 52, 55, 61, 83, 96, 97, 99, 103, 104–105

Jerry Heasley Collection: pp. 36, 71, 81, 82, 111

©Ron Kimball: pp. 26–27, 29, 84–85, 88, 90, 91, 92, 93, 94–95

©Daniel B. Lyons: pp. 8, 10, 21 bottom, 22, 30, 37, 43, 45 top, 66–67, 72, 87, 98, 110

©Mike Mueller: pp. 2, 6, 16 both, 18, 19, 38, 39 top, 40–41, 45 bottom, 46, 53, 56–57, 58, 59, 60 bottom, 95 right

Mike Mueller Collection: p. 54

National Motor Museum: ©Nicky Wright: pp. 64, 74–75, 78, 79